THE SAGA OF PA...

General George C. Kenney

First published by DUELL, SLOAN AND PEARCE in 1959.

This edition published in 2017.

TABLE OF CONTENTS

FOREWORD

THIS IS the story of an extraordinary character. Incidentally, he was one of the great heroes of the Southwest Pacific in World War II, a mechanical genius, and one of the finest story-tellers I have ever known. His deeds were real. His stories were often fantasies but they and the recital of his actual accomplishments will be told and retold as long as any of his comrades-in-arms are still alive and then will be handed down to succeeding generations of airmen. Pappy Gunn is already a legendary figure.

He was a spectacular person but spectacular things seemed to seek him out and highlight the fact that he was different. There was something strangely contagious about that difference which often communicated itself to anyone who came in close contact with him. He lived, died, and even was buried differently from other people.

His outstanding characteristic was devotion. He was devoted to his country, to the organization to which he belonged, to his commanders, and, above all, to those who served under him. His devotion to his family and his constant worry over their safety during their three years in a Japanese prison camp endeared him to his associates. Pappy didn't know it but they soon realized that his flamboyance, his quick temper, his reckless flying, and his astounding tales which had little to identify them with his actual accomplishments, were really just attempts to cover up the deep emotions which he did not wish to expose to the public gaze.

He was a fearless fighter who demonstrated his qualities of leadership by leading. To the youngsters fresh from the training fields and untried in air combat he was an example, an inspiration, a confidence builder, an invaluable man to have around. If any piece of equipment from the airplane itself to any of its hundreds of accessories failed to work, the universal answer was "Pappy can fix it," and Pappy could and did.

Generals, admirals, and privates have paid tribute to Pappy Gunn. They all praise his exploits and agree that he should be accorded a top spot on the list of aviation's pioneers — but they all speak of having lost a true friend.

His sister Jewell, however, pays him the greatest tribute of all.

"When the news came of Paul's death, it was such a blow that for a while I was numbed. I couldn't think. Then I remembered the many times he had told me that he wanted to be active and flying as long as he lived. I know he was happy in his work. It was his life.

"We were so proud of everything he accomplished and appreciated the honors that were conferred upon him.

"To me he was the best brother in the world."

Colonel Paul Irvin Gunn was admired, respected, and loved by his friends — I don't believe he ever had an enemy. Our country owes him a debt that his tragic death in an airplane accident in the Philippines on October 11, 1957, makes it impossible for us now ever to repay. Perhaps this story will help discharge a part of that debt by keeping alive the memory of a great character, a superb aviator, a devoted American husband and father — a man.

1. "PAPPY" AND THE WHALE

The Time — *mid-afternoon, July 28, 1943.*
The Place — *the Bismarck Sea just northeast of Cape Gloucester on the west end of the Island of New Britain.*
The Target — *two Japanese destroyers steaming west at full speed after being discovered by an American reconnaissance airplane.*

FOR NEARLY a week Lieutenant Colonel Paul I. "Pappy" Gunn had been at Three Mile Airdrome at Port Moresby, New Guinea, waiting for a chance to test our latest gun-airplane combination. It was a 75-millimeter cannon mounted in the nose of the B-25 or Mitchell bomber. Pappy had fallen in love with it as soon as he saw it, and begged me to let him test it against the first Jap vessel that came within range. I told him to join the 3rd Attack Group, my pet skip-bombing boys, and I would see that he got the first shot at the target. Pappy had been a member of that outfit before I attached him to my own staff and made him a Special Projects officer. The 3rd Group called him "The General's Uninhibited Engineer," but they were proud of his accomplishments and the unorthodox methods he used to attain them. They were sort of unorthodox themselves.

Shortly after noon, a radio flash from one of our reconnaissance planes gave us the news Pappy and the 3rd Group gang had been waiting for. With Gunn's B-25 in the lead, in fifteen minutes thirty-six bombers were on their way. The weather was spotty, with fairly large patches of rain areas and poor visibility, so the group broke up into three squadrons of twelve planes each and fanned out to cover a wide front and be sure of intercepting the two Jap ships. The planes cruised along just over the waves and islands and coral reefs, never over a hundred feet from the ground or water. These were the low-altitude boys who boasted that they didn't carry oxygen because they didn't fly high enough to use it and that if on a flight they came across a cow, they flew around it. They were also "the skip-bombing gang" who came roaring into the attack at wave-top altitude and skipped their bombs up against the sides of enemy vessels, hurdled the masts, and waited for the four-second delay fuses to detonate the bombs. In that brief time, traveling at nearly five hundred feet per second, they would get out of danger from being hit by their own bomb fragments or pieces of the enemy ship. It was a hair-raising type of attack, but it was succeeding beyond all our original expectations. Moreover, the 3rd Group had the lowest combat casualty record in the whole Fifth Air Force, and all the rest of the groups were busy training their crews to follow the 3rd's example.

Shortly after two-thirty, the squadron, with Pappy in the lead, broke through a rain squall into clear weather, and there dead ahead less than two miles away were the two Jap destroyers heading for a big fog bank about a mile to the west. There was no time to jockey for position, for the wake behind the vessels showed they were moving at top speed to get under cover. Pappy signaled for the attack and at a distance of 1,500 yards opened fire on the leading and largest of the two ships. He had six shells for his 75-millimeter gun. The projectile part, about three inches in diameter, weighed sixteen pounds, of which a pound and a half was TNT.

The first shot hit one of the destroyer's stacks, the second ricocheted along the deck knocking out an antiaircraft gun position. Number three missed altogether, and number four was square in the middle of the hull. Pappy was so close now that he had to pull up, hurdle the ship, and turn around for another pass. One trouble was that the destroyer didn't seem to pay any attention to that little three-inch hole and was still steaming along at a good thirty-five knots.

Pappy's two wingmen sized up the situation. There was only time for one more pass before the Jap ships would be getting under cover of the fog bank just ahead of them. They called Gunn on the radio. "Pappy, will you please get the hell out of the way and let us show you how a destroyer ought to be sunk." Pappy's reply, properly expurgated and considerably shortened, was "OK, you knuckle heads, I wish this obscene crock carried a few more rounds of ammunition. I'd show you." The conversation now fell on deaf ears as the two wingmen flying abreast with the throttles wide open, and their twenty-four forward-firing machine guns blazing, came in on the attack. At about two hundred yards from the Jap vessel, each dropped a five-hundred-pound bomb. The pair climbed steeply barely missing the masts and stacks. Two explosions accompanied by two clouds of mixed flame, smoke, and water with bits of debris obscured the destroyer and told the story even before things cleared up so that the results could be seen and entered in the report to be turned in after the return to the home airdrome. One bomb had blown the whole stern off. The other had penetrated the hull just above the water line, and when it detonated inside, had broken the ship in two. The two halves were already almost out of sight.

The squadron headed back home. The two wingmen swung in behind Pappy to let him lead the return flight. There were no more targets as the second destroyer had also been taken care of by some of the other members of the squadron. Pappy sulked and silently cursed the gang that had shown up both him and his pet gun installation that he had pinned such high hopes on.

As the twelve planes approached Cape Gloucester where the Japs had a little field, Pappy saw a chance to vindicate himself and restore his sunken prestige. A Jap transport plane had just landed and was taxiing along the strip. Skimming over the treetops Pappy's attack was a complete surprise. The first of the two remaining shells hit the right engine and the second exploded right in the pilot's cockpit. As he told me afterward, "General, when I passed over that wreck there were pieces of Jap higher than I was." Pappy's prestige was now restored. Nobody could kid him now about his new gun installation.

The squadron crossed over the west end of the island of New Britain, passed over a school of whales in the Solomon Sea to the south who looked as though they were playing a type of cetacean water polo, then swung over the eastern end of New Guinea and landed at their home field at Three Mile.

With their reports turned in, the crews lounged around the squadron operations room. They had already forgotten all about the war, and nobody wanted to chide Pappy for not sinking that destroyer. His sulphurous reply could easily set fire to the grass and palm-leaf-thatched operations hut and perhaps to the nearby jungle as well. One of the pilots decided to break the silence, but he would keep away from any dangerous reference to the mission they had just returned from.

"Say Pappy," he said, "did you see those whales we passed over in the Solomon Sea."

"Yeah," replied Pappy, "I saw them." Then his eyes suddenly seemed to light up, and he cleared his throat. The gang gathered around us as if a signal had been given. Pappy was about to tell one of his stories, and they weren't going to miss a word of it.

"You may not know it," said Pappy, "but the whale is the most intelligent of all animals. He not only has brains, but he's a friendly guy. He likes people and wants to do things for them. If he wasn't so damn big, he'd make a wonderful house pet.

"Those whales out there today reminded me of the time back in 1930 when I was flying in the Navy. It was during maneuvers off the north coast of Haiti. I was flying a catapult, pontoon job off the cruiser Omaha doing reconnaissance, hunting for the 'enemy' submarines.

"There I am one day at five thousand feet and about a hundred miles away from my ship, when all of a sudden the engine quits. I was quite sure I knew what it was. You see, in those days they used to put hose connections in the gas lines. Those old motors used to vibrate so, they were afraid the lines would break if they didn't give 'em some flexibility. Sometimes the gasoline would rot the rubber, and little bits of it would get in the line or in the carburettor and shut off the fuel from getting through to the engine. I knew what to do if I could just land without cracking up, but when I looked at the old Atlantic boiling away, I figured that when I did get down I was going to be lucky if I had anything left to sit on until I was rescued.

"I spiralled down looking for a wave that was maybe a little smoother than the others when all of a sudden when I'm about two hundred feet high, I see a beautiful wake into the wind just ahead of me.

"I landed in that wake, slide along nice and pretty, and then with just a hint of a jolt I stop. When I looked over the side to see what I had run into, damned if I wasn't on the back of a whale.

"I sat there for a while but the whale didn't move, so I said to myself, 'What the hell!' and got out and stood on the whale's back, lifted up the cowling, cleaned out the carburettor and gas lines, put on some new hose connections I had in my pocket, and buttoned the cowling up again. Then I got the crank for the inertia starter out of the plane, stood there with one foot on the whale and the other on a pontoon, and cranked away until I got the fly wheel spinning fast. Now I get into the cockpit, turn on the ignition, and let in the fly wheel clutch. The prop turns over, the engine takes, and I'm in business. Now the whale — remember I told you how smart they are — he knows I'm ready to go so he softly submerges being careful not to flick his tail and maybe hit the plane. About a hundred feet out ahead of me, he surfaces, turns into the wind, and gives it full power as he makes another long smooth wake for me to take off on and come back to the Omaha."

Pappy looked around grinning happily, waited a few seconds for the applause, which he got, and turned to go. "I guess I'd better see if Sergeant Evans has got that ship of mine ready to go out on another mission," he said and walked out of the hut toward the flying line.

2. A BOY'S DREAM

PAUL IRVIN "PAPPY" GUNN was born in Quitman, Arkansas, a little village of about eight hundred people some forty-five miles north of Little Rock, on October 18, 1900. If you check on his military records in the Pentagon in Washington, D.C., you will find the date of Pappy's birth is a year earlier, but that minor error is because of his desire to avoid embarrassing questions from the navy recruiting officer in Little Rock on August 8, 1917, the date of his first enlistment. The new recruit was not yet eighteen at that time and there probably would have been a matter of parental consent involved. Anyhow, the little discrepancy in giving the exact date of his birth was not important to Pappy then or from then on. His father, Nathaniel Hezekiah Gunn with his wife, Laura Litton Gunn, and their six children had moved to Quitman in 1896, bought fifty-five acres of land, and built a six-room frame house and a barn. In addition to farming and fruit growing, Nathaniel was a livestock dealer, buying cattle and driving them overland to Little Rock or to Kensett, a railroad-junction town fifty miles southeast of Quitman for shipment on the Missouri Pacific Railroad to the St. Louis market. Whenever the subject came up, "Pappy" always said his father was a mule skinner from the Ozark Mountains and that he had followed in his footsteps before enlisting in the Navy. The Gunns, like the rest of the local farmers, always had a span of mules. That probably furnished enough background for Pappy's story. In fact, it was more background than he generally needed on which to build the fantastic stories that his listeners looked forward to.

In August 1907 Nathaniel died. The five oldest children, Pearl, Lish, Dess, Dorris, and Claudine, by this time were all married and living away from home. Mrs. Gunn didn't feel that she could work the farm so she rented it and with the remaining four children, Jewell, now eleven, and the three new arrivals since the family had moved to Quitman, Charles, nine, Paul Irvin, seven, and Litton, five, moved to a small house in town. The following March, during a windy night, the house burned to the ground, the family barely escaping with little more than their nightclothes. That spring and summer, Laura and the children lived with her married daughter Claudine and two of the married sons, Dorris and Lish.

In the fall the family was reunited when Laura moved them to a farm near Lonoke, twenty-five miles east of Little Rock, where her brothers Jim and Charley Litton had plantations. The Gunn family lived there three years, growing cotton and some garden truck. A hired man did the ploughing and the family did the planting, hoeing, and gathering of the crops. The school system was adjusted to fit the farm schedule. The one-room schoolhouse took care of the first six grades. A three-month term in winter and another three months in summer gave the youngsters time to do the spring planting and cultivating and gather the crops in the fall when the cotton had to be picked and carted to the gin in Lonoke.

It was on one of these trips to town one day in 1908 that Charley and Paul decided to walk home. They had just started when an automobile, the first one they had ever seen, overtook them. The driver stopped and offered them a lift. The two open-mouthed lads got aboard too overcome to do anything but nod their consent. In grand style, to the astonishment of the neighbours and consternation of the chickens and livestock, they arrived in front of their house, and, getting out, ran to their mother standing on the front porch. After the car had gone and the dust settled they discovered that one of their pigs was lying in the road dead. The topic of conversation for the next month or two had nothing to do with the loss of the pig. The great adventure in the wonderful automobile was told and retold by Paul on every occasion, and each time it was a better story with more and more emphasis on the size, power, and speed of the car. He had decided that someday he was going to drive one of those things.

His ambition lasted until the fall of 1910 when one day, while the family was in the cotton field, an airplane flew overhead. Paul, then a thin, wiry, blue-eyed kid of ten, watched until it was out of sight, then turned to his mother and said, "Someday I'm going to fly like that." This was the dream that he now began to live. He liked to draw. At first automobiles and later airplanes appeared in chalk on fences and the sides of the barn. His teachers encouraged and helped him, and it wasn't long before his pen-and-ink sketches and drawings of airplanes in considerable detail began to adorn the walls of his room. He read everything that mentioned aviation and talked about flying constantly, sometimes to the amusement of the neighbours but more often with much shaking of heads and thankfulness that their youngsters didn't have such crazy ideas as that Gunn boy. The rest of his family tolerated Paul's enthusiasm but certainly did not share or approve of his dreams of someday becoming an aviator.

In 1911 the family moved back to Quitman. The town located at the edge of the Ozarks was on higher ground than Lonoke and had a much more healthful climate. The "chills and fever" of the latter location was getting to be too much for them, so Laura moved back to the old farm and the frame house Nathaniel had built fifteen years before.

They didn't have any recognition in those days for "Mother of the Year." If they had had, Laura would have been a real contestant. The four youngsters now ranging from Litton's nine years to Jewell's fifteen helped her to run the farm, but the main burden fell on Laura, who had determined to make good citizens of all of them. It would add to her work, but they must be educated and brought up to be a credit to her and the community. Her own religious instruction supplemented that of the Sunday school and the church. Ploughing, seeding, cultivating, gathering crops, and building up the insatiable woodpile for cooking and heating took a lot of the family's time, but Laura saw to it that they attended school whenever they could be spared. Many times she carried the load herself so that they wouldn't miss an important class or an examination.

She believed in discipline and the old idea that children should be obedient, respectful, and law-abiding. If necessary, and when talking did not bring the desired results, she was prepared to use the rod rather than spoil the child. Paul used to recall, when talking about his mother, whom he adored, an occasion when he had shirked a hoeing job to go fishing. When he returned home proudly displaying a good string of fish, Laura invited him into the smokehouse where she kept a peach-tree switch. Unfortunately for the lesson in discipline she forgot to shut the door before Paul's dog, Shep, came in to see what was happening to his master. Paul's exaggerated yells were too much for Shep. The punishment had to be called off while Paul rescued his mother. However, as he always ended the story, "The next time and from then on, Mother always remembered to close the smokehouse door before she reached for the switch."

Laura's system evidently worked. The youngsters got an education and were described by their neighbours as a healthy, well-behaved, and industrious family.

One of his former teachers, Edna Clark, now Mrs. J. K. Graves of Mineral Wells, Texas, says of Paul:

"I remember him very well. I knew him as a typical American boy. I was his teacher three years, about 1914 through 1916 in the third, fourth, and fifth grades. He was a good average student, regular in attendance, and he seemed to enjoy the school activities. He liked to draw and he memorized poems very well. I thought a great deal of him as a student and he seemed to like me."

The children all worshiped their mother and did all they could to ease her burden of running the farm and keeping the family properly fed and clothed. In his spare time Paul shined shoes at the local barbershop and joined the others in picking blackberries which they sold to the neighbours. The money was always turned over to their mother to help with expenses in spite of the fact that she almost invariably returned it to them for spending money. There was no drugstore soda fountain in Quitman then but the town youngsters had an acceptable substitute at Martin's Grocery Store where "Uncle" Rollie used to mix up huge ice-cold milk shakes of all flavours. The price — five cents.

The big annual event in Quitman in those days was the Fourth-of-July picnic in the park on the edge of town. It was the homecoming day when people saw friends and relatives they hadn't seen for months or even years. Among the games, races, and other events one of the regular attractions was the climbing of a greased pole about fifteen feet long, hanging from a scaffold with the bottom of the pole about three feet from the ground and a five-dollar bill donated by the local banker at the top.

It was after lunch before the work on the farm was done and Laura and the four children, dressed in their Sunday best, arrived at the park. A dozen contestants had already failed to climb the greased pole. When Paul arrived, his cheering schoolmates and friends around town insisted that he show them how it should be done.

Paul looked the situation over, felt of the pole, and said, "Wait till I go home and get my overalls and I'll give it a try." He was back in a few minutes. Three times he almost made it to the accompanying cheers, laughter, and good-natured bantering of the crowd, but finally he reached the top, grabbed the bill, and slid back to the ground greasy and dirty but triumphant. When the family returned home that evening, Paul got his mother aside, handed her the five-dollar bill, and said, "Here, Mother, will you take this and buy a hundred-pound sack of sugar and make a whole lot of that blackberry jelly I like?"

World War I broke out in August 1914. Soon the papers began carrying stories about British, French, and German fliers dashing through the skies shooting at each other. They were the new knights-errant. The word "ace," denoting a pilot who had downed five or more enemy planes, crept into our vocabulary. Paul knew every one of the stories of these daredevils and their achievements by heart and when in April 1917 the United States entered the war he had already made up his mind. He would enlist and become a flier. The crops were planted and the summer term about to begin at the Quitman school. That would delay him another three months and anyhow he had enough education. He had completed the fifth grade and part of the sixth.

With one of his school chums, George M. Hooten, Paul left for Little Rock on one of the freight wagons. George says they told everyone they were going to the big city to make their fortune.

To get a little money to live on while they looked the recruiting situation over, the two boys got jobs at an ice-cream dairy where they worked for a couple of months and then quit to work for an insurance company. In the meantime they investigated the relative advantages and opportunities open to them in the Army, the Navy, and the Marines. The navy prospects looked best, so on August 8, 1917, that service signed up two new recruits. George Hooten enlisted as a musician and Paul Irvin Gunn for Naval Aviation. That night he wrote home and told his mother that he had enlisted in the Navy and was going to become a flier. It didn't come as a surprise to her. She had been aware for some time that Paul wanted aviation as a career more than anything else in the world. The older youngsters shook their heads, but Laura said, "Paul has a will of his own and I will not interfere with his wishes." She was worried, of course, but she had a lot of faith in his ability and had always taught him not to quit doing anything simply because it was hard, but to keep on trying and eventually he would find out how to accomplish it. She was not going to go back on her teaching now. The neighbours' comments varied from "Paul is too adventurous for his own good" to "Too bad he is worrying his poor mother so," "He is just throwing his life away," and "The boy is just crazy." The next day he left for New Orleans for his three months' course in basic training.

3. A DREAM FULFILLED

IN MID-NOVEMBER 1917 Paul was sent to the naval air base at Pensacola, Florida. He was probably destined to be sent there anyway after completing the "boot-camp" or basic course at New Orleans, but later he insisted that they sent him there to get rid of him. According to his story, after a month or two of basic training he had been assigned to the camp kitchen for duty. One day the cook told him to make up a batch of tapioca pudding. Paul didn't know anything about making this dessert except that it had tapioca in it, and to make sure that there would be enough for the garrison of around two hundred hungry recruits he put all the tapioca in the kitchen in the biggest pot he could find and set it on the big range to cook. His stories of the disaster that followed never lessened in the horrible details. The last time I heard the tale, the tapioca swelled and boiled over until it completely covered the stove and was several inches deep on the floor. Paul was put to work with a hammer and chisel to remove the burned mess from the stove, but for three days the command had to eat cold food before the kitchen was restored to normal. He always claimed that was how he lost his cook's job and got transferred to Pensacola.

After a short furlough back home in the spring of 1918, where he regaled his family and the whole town with stories of flying, and proudly exhibited snapshots of airplanes with himself in or near them, Seaman Second-Class Paul Gunn left for the Great Lakes Training School near Chicago to take the aviation mechanics course. He never seemed to realize that there would be any difficulty in getting flying training as an enlisted man. He had decided that he was going to be a pilot and somehow he was going to make it. That fall he finished his mechanics course and was sent back to Pensacola with the rating of machinist's mate first class.

Now that he was regularly assigned to the flying line everything seemed all right, but soon another interference with his desire to spend all his time around airplanes loomed up. As a boy he had liked music and had become quite proficient with a trombone that someone had given him. At the time of his enlistment in 1917, back in Little Rock, in answer to some question in the recruiting office, he had admitted his liking for music and that he could play a trombone. Now, at Pensacola, Paul suddenly found himself detailed to the base orchestra. The assignment didn't disturb him until he found that a lot of the practicing was done in the afternoon. He knew by this time that nothing would be gained by protesting about this new job so he solved his problem in his own typical way.

One evening at a dance on the base Paul and his trombone were a part of the musical program. In those days there were few or no variations in the prevalent waltz and two-step music. At one of the pauses in the number then being played Paul decided something was needed to change the monotony. There followed a sound closely resembling the waah-huh-waah-huh laughing of a donkey. His astonished fellow musicians stopped playing, the dancers stopped dancing, and Paul stopped being a member of the base orchestra by order of the senior naval officer present. The reprimand that followed the next day might have bothered anyone else, but when he was informed that he would have to do a week's extra duty on the flying line for punishment, Paul humbly said, "Yes, sir," saluted, and withdrew. His method of getting back to his beloved airplanes had been somewhat unusual but he had won. To him that was all that mattered.

When World War I ended on November 11, 1918, Paul had already decided to stay in the Navy. He still had to get that pair of gold wings on his chest. He was now eighteen years old, about five feet ten, a thin, wiry, blue-eyed, likable kid with unbounded energy and the reputation of knowing more about the mechanics of fixing airplanes and engines than anyone else on the base. Of course the navy records showed him to be nineteen, but Paul didn't worry about such things. It was better to let sleeping dogs lie.

Patience, however, was never one of his virtues. If he couldn't get flying training with the Navy, he would get it by himself. Other people could go to town on a pass and have fun but that cost money. He scrimped and saved his pay and began taking private lessons from a local civilian gypsy flier on weekends when he could get away from the base. Once in a while he would get in a little extra flying time in return for helping as a mechanic keeping the airplane in shape.

By the spring of 1922 Paul had soloed and now had his own airplane, an old single-engine d Curtiss Seagull flying boat left over from World War I which had been junked and surveyed by the Navy. It cost him $250.00. After hours and on Sundays he worked on it, patched it up, getting the engine in working order, and finally got it flying. Where the tools, spare parts, and materials came from is one of those still-unsolved mysteries.

Up to this time girls were distractions that interfered with his dream but perhaps because he had finally realized at least part of his goal, romance for something besides an airplane entered the picture. One night as a stag at a dance at the Odd Fellows Hall in town Paul, now a handsome lad of twenty-three, noticed a good-looking, slim, dark-haired girl about five feet two whom he decided he wanted to meet. As she waltzed by he tagged her escort, introduced himself, and dated her up for the next evening. Incidentally, just before returning her to her escort he asked her what her name was. He thought it would be a good idea to know whom he was calling on. She agreed. Her name was Clara Louise Crosby whose father was a local contractor and cabinetmaker. She was then twenty years old.

As Paul left her the next evening he casually remarked that he liked her and wanted to see a lot of her but not to get any funny ideas about a wedding as he had made up his mind not to get married until he was forty. It doesn't seem to have discouraged Clara Louise although this warning was repeated at practically every one of the frequent dates they had for nearly a year. In the meantime, Paul had decided that he liked "Polly" as a name better than Clara Louise and it became Polly from then on. One day out of the blue Paul, or P.I. as Polly now called him, suddenly said, "Polly, let's get married."

"When?" was Polly's reply.

"Now," said Paul.

Polly wanted to wait a while longer, and the pair finally set the date for June 7, 1923, when the knot was tied and the couple took off that afternoon in Paul's flying boat for Biloxi, Mississippi, about one hundred miles west of Pensacola. They had been there about a week when flying along the coast just off Biloxi Paul saw the body of a man on the beach of one of the sandy islands in that area. He flew back to Biloxi, pulled into the beach, told Polly to mind the plane, and hurried over to the local police station to report his discovery.

The chief of police listened sceptically to Paul's story and finally said, "Look, sailor, why can't you and your wife just keep on enjoying your honeymoon and leave the police business to us?"

"But," protested Paul, "there's a corpse out there on that island."

"Sure, sure." The police chief tried to calm Paul down and get rid of him. Paul finally lost his temper. "You act as if you didn't believe me, but if any of you knuckle heads have guts enough to fly with me, I'll take you out there and show you."

The police chief finally gave in and let Paul fly him out to the island, leaving Polly behind. "You'd better go on back to the hotel and wait for me," said Paul. "This might be kind of messy."

In a little while they returned with the corpse and Paul was not only vindicated but on the way to becoming a local celebrity, which didn't suit him at all. The next day, after vainly trying to dodge newspapermen and townspeople wanting to talk to him about the occurrence, Paul said, "Polly, we can't have any privacy here; let's go." That afternoon they flew back to Pensacola. The honeymoon was over and Paul went back to his job as machinist's mate at the naval base.

The navy records show that his first six-year enlistment was up on August 7, 1924, but they also show that on August 8, 1924, he signed up for a second six-year tour. Congress had passed a rider to the Appropriation Bill calling for training qualified enlisted men as well as officers as airplane pilots. Paul had been promised that he was qualified and would be given the navy flying training course if he re-enlisted.

In the spring of 1925 he had completed his flying instruction and received his gold wings with the rating of CAP or Chief Airplane Pilot. The dream had been fulfilled.

4. NAVAL AVIATOR

PAUL AND POLLY'S first child, a girl christened Constance, was born in 1924 while her father was starting his flying training. At this time the family was living outside the naval base in Pensacola in a little house that Paul and Polly's father had built together in their spare time. In 1926, about the time the Navy obviated the chance of CAP Gunn being mistaken for a captain by changing the rating to AP, or Airplane Pilot, the second child, another girl, Julie, joined the growing Gunn family.

That year Paul was transferred to the naval base at San Diego, California, where he did a two-year tour before being transferred back to Pensacola where for five months, from August through December of 1928, he was an instructor at the naval flying school. Many a navy pilot, some of them destined to high rank in World War II, remember vividly the tough but thorough instruction they got from Airplane Pilot Instructor Gunn and the picturesque language that accompanied his remarks about their slowness in absorbing his words of wisdom.

Rank meant little to Paul then. Twenty-five years later, when he served under me, it was quite evident that even twenty years of navy service had not spoiled his God-given confidence in himself and his complete intolerance of the "knuckle heads" who did not understand or disagreed with him. At the same time you never thought of insubordination in connection with Gunn. He was too likable and too loyal to get annoyed with, and, furthermore, he had a genius for accomplishment in connection with anything to do with an airplane. I remember putting on one of his efficiency ratings the notation: "This officer gets things done." I couldn't think of any higher compliment to pay him.

While Paul was on this five-months temporary duty at Pensacola, Polly, who had followed him back from San Diego with the two children, stayed at the little house her father and Paul had started building three years before. There was a reason for her staying home, as their third child, a boy this time, named Paul after his father, arrived in late 1928.

Right after the first of the year 1929 Paul, senior, was transferred to Anacostia Naval Air Station near Washington, D.C., where he served as an airplane pilot for two years. The executive officer at the station was Lieutenant Commander Joseph J. "Jocko" Clark who, as Rear Admiral

Clark, became a famous Task Force Commander during World War II. He and Paul evidently became fast friends. This is what Admiral Clark says of him:

"In those days Anacostia had the task of flying many important government officials around the country and therefore we wanted the best pilots we could get. With the whole Navy to draw on, we picked P. I. Gunn. In those days we called him 'P. I.' — he got the nickname of 'Pappy' later.

"He was exceptionally able, always ready to go anywhere any time — day or night. He had a cheerful and inspiring personality and a high sense of duty. Of our team of pilots, he was universally regarded as a crack member.

"Once, in the spring of 1929, I think it was, P. I. and I made a flight to Detroit and back in a Fairchild high-wing monoplane. I flew the plane up there and he flew back. As we passed over Cleveland we encountered a dense fog. This was before the days of reliable weather instruments and before any all-weather flying. We lost sight of the ground and saw nothing but fog until we got a quick glimpse of the McKeesport Air Field which appeared under us. This is near Pittsburgh. There was not enough ceiling to make a safe landing, so we kept on going.

"P. I. passed me the map. While he concentrated on flying the plane, I spotted a road which I recognized to be the road from Pittsburgh to Uniontown. I told him to 'stay with the road.' He did a superb job, even though the tops of the trees were frequently cut off as we crossed the ridges. The road brought us eventually into Uniontown, where we had enough ceiling to land and wait for clear weather. It took sheer guts and precision flying to stay with that road."

During this tour of duty in 1930 the fourth child, another son named Nathaniel after his paternal grandfather, was born. Soon after Nathaniel arrived, the Gunns moved back to Pensacola and their little home outside the naval base.

Polly and the four youngsters didn't see much of Paul for the next two years as he was doing his tour of sea duty. He was assigned to the cruiser Omaha, from which he was catapulted off in a float plane doing reconnaissance missions during the navy exercises and manoeuvres. On August 8, 1930, in the middle of his sea duty, he signed up for his third six-year enlistment. He had decided on Naval Aviation as a career for at least twenty years, when he would be eligible for half-pay retirement.

Most of Paul's flying during this tour was in the Caribbean and the Atlantic where Pappy landed on the whale, but in the fall of 193 1 he was flying over the Pacific in manoeuvres off Hawaii. A double hernia that he always insisted he got from frequent catapulting put him in the naval hospital in Hawaii. On his discharge he was ordered back to his former station at San Diego, where Polly and the four children met him and where they remained until 1933.

Just after his transfer Paul received word that his mother was desperately ill and not expected to live. At this time, with all her children married, she had given up the farm in Quitman and was living with her daughter Jewell, now Mrs. Has Owen, in the little town of Searcy, about twenty miles southeast of the old Gunn place.

Paul got an emergency leave, wired that he was on the way, and with another sailor who was going East, drove day and night all the way from San Diego to Searcy. When Laura heard that Paul was coming she seemed to rally and by the time he arrived, seemed much better. She enjoyed every minute of the visit and asked Paul all about his family and particularly about his flying.

Two days later she was so much better that Paul decided to go back to San Diego. Before leaving he asked his mother if there was anything he could do or get for her. Laura smiled and said, "I'd like some peppermint-stick candy like you used to bring me when you were a little boy." Paul kept the lump in his throat down and said, "All right, Mother, I'll get some right away."

A little later he took the candy to her. She smiled up at him as he kissed her good-by for the last time. After he left, the tears came. Laura said, "I couldn't let him see me cry this last time. I can cry after he's gone." The rally, however, was merely a temporary respite induced by her joy in seeing her favourite and most glamorous son again. When Paul arrived back at San Diego he was informed that his mother had died while he was en route.

The transfer back to San Diego was not entirely accidental. Commander "Jocko" Clark had been assigned to that station and had pulled a few strings for his old flying partner. He says this about the incident:

"When I left Anacostia I made sure that P. I. was transferred to my next assignment which was command of VF 2, the old Fighting Squadron Two, operating from the old aircraft carrier Lexington, which sank at the Battle of the Coral Sea. VF 2 was known as the 'Enlisted Men's Squadron' because with the exception of the section leaders, who were officers, the pilots were all enlisted men. Competition was very keen on the part of the navy enlisted pilots to get assigned to VF 2. Only the best were selected for this duty.

"For two years P. I. was my right-wing man. He was an excellent aerial gunner, and at aerial combat, which was our main mission, he was rated as one of the very best in the squadron.

"One dark night, when the squadron was returning from the Lexington at sea, where we had qualified in night landings, to the naval air station at San Diego, we encountered a solid fog bank off Point Lanea. P. I. got caught in the soup and his plane went into a spin. Only his persistent determination enabled him to right the plane a few feet off the water."

That was a famous squadron in those days. We used to call it the Top Hat Squadron, and they deserved the title. You had to be a red-hot pilot to be a member of the Top Hats. Airplane Pilot Paul I. Gunn was that good.

In 1933 he was again transferred to the naval air base in Hawaii at Pearl Harbor where he flew with the base squadron and was in charge of aircraft and engine maintenance.

From time to time the Lexington would visit Pearl Harbor on manoeuvres, and Paul would be welcomed by his old squadron mates and get a chance to fly with them.

In addition to its reputation for precision flying in formation and acrobatics the squadron gained a lot of attention when, for more than a week, its pilots combed the South Pacific looking for Amelia Earhart whose airplane had vanished on July 2, 1937, on an attempted flight from Port Moresby, New Guinea, to Howland Island on her proposed flight around the world. Paul was one of those on the search who flew themselves almost to exhaustion looking for some sign of the missing aircraft. What actually happened to Amelia Earhart and her navigator Fred Noonan is still a mystery. No trace of the airplane or its occupants was ever found.

It was about this time that an incident occurred that was typical of Paul's whole career. Anything that bothered him or interfered with what he was trying to do annoyed him and had to be brushed aside. If he broke any rules or regulations in the process, that was something to worry about later. People who didn't agree with him, unless he liked them a lot, were "knuckle heads," generally with supplementary adjectives.

For years his teeth had been giving him trouble, but after a couple of experiences in having them drilled and filled, he had decided that dentists were a bunch of unskilled mechanics who shouldn't be trusted with an overhaul job on his mouth. He did condescend, one morning, to ask the navy dentist at the base to pull all his teeth and make him, what Paul called, "a set of broken dishes." The dentist refused to carry out Paul's wish and made a date with him to come in a few days later on for some dental work.

Paul said, "All right, I'll be seeing you," got a pass for the afternoon, hunted up a Japanese civilian dentist in Honolulu, and told him what he wanted. The Jap took a cast of his mouth, worked all the afternoon making up a complete set of false teeth, and that evening extracted all of Paul's teeth. For the next few days he lived on soft food but kept on the job working on airplanes and taking his turn flying without saying a word about either the teeth he had just lost or the new ones he was breaking in. The navy dentist ran into him one day and wanted to know why Paul hadn't been in to see him. Paul grinned, took out his new teeth, and said, "They don't ache anymore and I don't see any cavities in them so I decided not to bother you." The astonished dentist shook his head and walked away muttering to himself something to the effect that all aviators were crazy but that some were crazier than others. Whether or not he ever made an official report of Paul's failure to get permission to go to a civilian dentist or not the records do not show, but the story of Airplane Pilot Gunn's teeth was told and retold for months all over the base.

Throughout his whole military career, Paul's commanding officers somehow seemed to have remembered him. As a matter of fact, you couldn't very well serve in the same outfit or on the same station with him and not remember him. However, I have never met anyone who did not speak favourably of him. They all liked him as a person, admired his ability as a pilot and all-around mechanical genius, and valued him as a friend.

Admiral J. W. "Black Jack" Reeves, Jr., and one of the old-time naval aviators, now retired, was first executive and then commanding officer of the Fleet Air Base on Ford Island in Pearl Harbor during 1937 and 1938. He and Paul worked together quite closely officially and became fast personal friends besides.

Admiral Reeves says, "Paul and I were fishing partners. We usually went out a couple of nights a week along the Ford Island shores. We used a small boat with one of us poling while the other stood in the bow with a three-pronged spear, spotting fish in the glare of a lantern secured to an old flying helmet and powered by an auto battery. This arrangement was surprisingly productive in the matter of fish on the table.

"P. I. was one of those old-time navy men who knew what the job was and aimed to do it up to the hilt. He was hard-headed, but who is worth his salt who is swayed like a tree in the wind?

"Personally he was a good companion whose friendship I valued then and always shall."

On August 6, 1937, Paul had completed twenty years' service. He retired as an airplane pilot with the rank of chief petty officer. His retired pay was a monthly check from his Uncle Sam for the princely sum of $110.

He had not retired without a lot of heavy thinking. He liked the Navy, he was still wildly enthusiastic about flying. And he liked the challenge of pitting his own skill and confidence in his own ability against the weather, the dangers of engine failure, and the difficulties of over-water navigation. The restrictions of military life had never bothered Paul. He took them all lightly, and while often skating close to real trouble, he had always managed to grin, bluff, and work his way out of his difficulties.

During his Hawaiian tour of duty with the Navy, Paul had become acquainted with two men, Bob Tyce, an old civilian pilot, and a man named Knox who had started the K-T Inter Island Flying Service. Paul used to spend weekends with them instructing their pilots and maintenance men and incidentally teaching Knox himself how to fly. On retirement, he now became superintendent of maintenance and in addition did a large part of the test flying of the Douglas DC-3's the line was equipped with. From time to time he also took his turn on regular chartered passenger, mail, and freight runs between the Islands.

Back in 1933 Paul had noticed a young recruit named Dan Stickle who had been assigned as one of his crew members. Dan liked airplanes, too, liked to work for Paul, and seemed to have a natural aptitude for his job. He and Gunn became fast friends and through Paul's influence Dan took all the courses in aviation engineering that the naval station offered, including a year specializing in overhaul of engines, carburettors, and ignition systems.

Dan's four-year enlistment was up shortly after Paul had retired. Dan didn't want to re-enlist, so after the two had talked things over Dan went to work for Paul as shop superintendent for the K-T Flying Service.

In 1939, while still with Inter Island Airways as they were now known, he met Andres Soriano of Manila, the head of the powerful Ayala family of the Philippines. Soriano had a twin-engined Beechcraft and wanted a pilot to fly it. Paul took the job toward the end of 1939 and went to Manila. Polly and the children went back home to Pensacola for three months until Paul sent for them, and the family, once more united, settled down in a nice little house in the suburb of Paranaque near Nichols Field, the airport of Manila.

By this time Paul had persuaded Soriano to back an airline to cover the Philippines. Named the Philippine Air Lines, it was originally financed by Soriano and Elizalde and Company, another branch of the Ayala family. Later on, in 1941, when the Philippine government took over 51 per cent of the stock, the Soriano and Elizalde interests controlled the remainder.

Gunn always referred to any organization he was connected with as his own and of course always referred to the Philippine Air Lines as "my airline," but actually he never owned any part of it.

Dan Stickle remained with Inter Island Airways when Paul went to Manila with Soriano, but there was an understanding between these two friends that if an airline there became a reality, Dan would follow him. In the summer of 1940 Stickle reported to Gunn, who gave him the job of superintendent of maintenance for the Philippine Air Lines.

5. PAPPY JOINS THE ARMY AIR FORCE IN THE PHILIPPINES

WHEN THE JAPS struck at Pearl Harbor on December 7, 1941, "Pappy," as he had been nicknamed by the younger pilots in the Air Force around Manila who looked upon him as an old-timer in the flying game, was operations manager of Philippine Air Lines looking after the three twin-engined Beechcraft and one twin-engined Sikorsky amphibian which was all the equipment the company possessed.

A few days previously the Navy had notified Pappy and his superintendent of maintenance, Dan Stickle, that they wanted both of them back on active duty. Besides persuading Dan to come out to Manila and do the maintenance job, Pappy had taught him how to fly. One of the first bits of news to come out of Hawaii after the Jap attack told them of the death of their old friend and employer, Bob Tyce. He was the first man killed on Oahu that Sunday morning. He had been standing in front of the K-T Flying Service hangar when the first attack hit. The Japs got him on the first pass.

On December 8, 1941, Manila time, December 7, at Pearl Harbor, General Brereton, commanding the Army Air Force in the Philippines, took over control of the Philippine Air Lines equipment and two other twin-engined Beechcraft of the Philippine Air Force. At the same time Pappy and Dan were ordered to report to the headquarters at Fort McKinley. There the adjutant general told them to hold up their right hands and swore them into the United States Army Air Force. Written orders commissioning them in the Army and assigning them to duty would be sent to them later, as soon as the headquarters could get around to it. Luckily the two wrote down their serial numbers on scraps of paper and then committed them to memory. It turned out to be their main identification later on, as between the confusion incident to the Jap attack and the evacuation of the headquarters soon after neither Gunn nor Stickle ever received written confirmation of their swearing in on December 8, 1941.

Pappy came in as a captain and Dan as a first lieutenant. The two astounded former navy men suddenly found that their allegiance had been transferred to another service, but, as Pappy said, "What the hell difference does it make? We're in the war."

Their next instructions were to take over and operate the air-transport equipment, ferrying military personnel, carrying official mail, dispatches, drugs, food, and other freight which needed to be moved in a hurry. That first day Jap air attacks on the Manila airdrome at Nichols Field destroyed the Sikorsky amphibian and shot up the two Beechcraft airplanes belonging to the Philippine Air Force. Pappy decided he'd better get a field of his own to operate from. There was not enough anti-aircraft artillery to go around, so he knew he wouldn't get any of it. It was up to him to select some place that the Japs wouldn't suspect.

A few years before there was a small field just west of the Chinese cemetery in the suburb of Grace Park that had once been used by the old Air Taxi Company since bought out by Philippine Air Lines. It had not been used for some time and the cemetery had grown around it, even incorporating the cinder runways in its driveway pattern. Pappy decided this was the place. His subsequent actions were undoubtedly irregular but he was pressed for time. It would have taken days or even weeks to get condemnation proceedings through, and anyway Pappy never did think about bothering other people and asking too many questions when he could do the job himself. He simply knocked down a few tombstones and monuments, just enough to give wing clearance, moved his planes, equipment, and maintenance people in, and without any fanfare went to work. Whether or not the Japs were superstitious about bothering graveyards the fact remained that Pappy never lost a plane from his improvised "airdrome."

He had two pilots to help on the job, Harold G. "Buzz" Slingsby formerly with Consolidated Aircraft, who had been ferrying PBY flying boats from the United States to the Dutch East Indies and Louis James Connelly of the Philippine Air Lines. At the outbreak of the war both had been mobilized and sworn in as lieutenants. Together with Pappy, they did the flying in the improvised air transport squadron. Dan Stickle took charge of maintenance. One of Dan's first accomplishments was to make one flyable airplane out of the two Philippine Air Force Beechcraft that had been wrecked by the Jap bombers. This gave Pappy four to work with. The flying was all of the hair-raising kind, at treetop altitude, most of it at night and in bad weather to avoid being spotted and shot down by the Jap fighters who controlled the air. They had practically wiped out the United

States and Philippine Air Forces on the opening day of the war, except for eighteen B-17 bombers that had been at Del Monte Field on the big southern island of Mindanao and which continued to operate until December 24, 1941, when the fourteen still remaining were ordered to Australia for overhaul and replacement of parts worn out or damaged in combat.

The four airplanes of Pappy's "Air Transport Service" became three a few days after the war broke out, when one of them was shot up by Jap strafers on the ground at Bataan where Connelly had landed it with some supplies for our infantry there. Pappy flew over and picked him up together with all the useful parts he could salvage, to use as spares to keep the remaining three flying.

Knowing the Philippines like a book from his past flyings over the island group, Pappy carried more than his share of the load. He always kept low, practically on the treetops or almost touching the water, to keep from even showing a shadow. His mechanics used to say that Captain Gunn brought leaves and seaweed home when he returned from a mission.

On December 13, 1941, Pappy was alone in his airplane coming back to Manila from Del Monte, where he had taken a load of staff officers and some serum and vaccines. Just before dark he was flying through the narrow valley that cuts across the northeast end of Cebu Island, when a Jap Zero spotted him and filled the plane full of lead. Luckily the engine kept running and the control cables were still intact. Pappy took it down among the bushes and grass and somehow managed to lose the Jap fighter. The plane was just barely manageable by this time but Pappy nursed it along, heading for his airdrome at Grace Park. On the way he passed over Zablan Field, the home base of the Philippine Air Force, and got shot up again by anti-aircraft machine gunners who thought he was a Jap. It was long after dark, and Pappy couldn't signal them, as both his radio and his landing lights had been knocked out when the Jap Zero attacked him over Cebu.

The plane had been in bad shape before, but this second barrage of machine-gun bullets had really fixed things. The motor started missing badly, and from the smell of gasoline Pappy figured his fuel tank had probably been hit so he turned west and headed for Nichols Field a couple of miles away. He barely made it, crash landing there in a black-out about ten o'clock at night. With the bits and pieces salvaged from the other two wrecks, Pappy and Dan Stickle patched the plane up, and three days later the command once again had three airplanes.

About this time Pappy was sent for by General Brereton and told to get one of his airplanes ready to evacuate President Quezon of the Philippines, his wife, two children, and one or two of his personal staff to Mindanao where a submarine would pick them up and take them to Australia. Pappy and Dan, the only one he took into his confidence, worked all night and most of the next day getting the airplane ready, but at the last minute General MacArthur decided to send the Quezon party all the way to Australia by a submarine which had just arrived in Manila Harbor.

Christmas Eve Pappy came in to the little house in Paranaque the Gunn family was living in, tossed a big roll of bills in Polly's lap, and told her that he had been ordered to ferry a load of passengers to Australia. He was leaving immediately and had come to say good-by for a while. The money was to keep things going until he returned. He had drawn all the pay due him and borrowed the rest.

He told Polly what everyone in the Philippines seems to have believed at the time, that in three weeks substantial army and navy forces would reinforce MacArthur and start running the Japs out of the country. Pappy said he expected to be back in about ten days or two weeks. However, he told Polly, if anything should go wrong, if reinforcements did not come, and the Japs should take over, not to tell them that her husband was flying for the Americans. She of course would have to admit that he had joined the Army but to say that he had been killed. She mustn't say that he had been shot down, as the Japs might have a record of it. She was just to say that Pappy had accidentally crashed in the water on a flight and the body never recovered. His final admonition was that if things went wrong and the Japs did come to Manila, she was to forget all about him until the Americans returned. He said he would not be able to get any messages through to her. He believed that if he did try to communicate with Polly in the event she was in the hands of the Japs, any messenger would be caught, the information tortured out of him, and his wife treated worse than ever.

As a matter of fact, this very thing did happen many times to the internees and prisoners the Japs held in Manila and to the messengers who tried to smuggle information to them.

General MacArthur had already ordered the remaining fourteen B-17 bombers flown to Australia together with as many extra pilots and mechanics as they could carry. By December 25, 1941, our bomber strength had dwindled to eleven. One was at Del Monte needing a tail wheel, a propeller, and some work done on the engine. Of the remaining ten at Darwin only three were in commission. Pappy's little Air Transport outfit was assigned to help out to the limit of its capacity. Shortly after midnight, on Christmas Day, the exodus began. "Buzz" Slingsby flew one of the Beechcraft and Pappy Gunn took the other, each with five passengers. Two days later they arrived in Darwin, Australia, and then went on to Brisbane where some newly arrived American air units were being assembled.

On January 2, 1942, the Japs entered Manila. Polly and the four children went into the University of Santo Tomas as internees to remain there until that day in February 1945, more than three years later, when the troops of the American 1st Cavalry Division broke into the university grounds and liberated them.

Pappy's friend and maintenance expert, Dan Stickel, was also picked up by the Japs. When Pappy left, he told Dan to report to Colonel H. H. George, the commanding officer of the Interceptor Command who was succeeding General Brereton as head of our Air Force in the Philippines. Brereton also left on Christmas Day for Java by order of General MacArthur. George told Dan to round up all the flyable P-40 fighter planes at Clark Field, about sixty miles north of Manila, and get them to Bataan. In early January Dan was picked up by a Jap patrol at Clark Field. He wasn't wearing any insignia. He didn't own any. The Japs evidently believed his story that he was a civilian mechanic and after keeping him a few days in Bilibid Prison with the military prisoners, transferred him to the internment camp at Santo Tomas University with the civilians.

Pappy from now on had two wars on his hands — the official one that his country was engaged in against Japan, and his own private war. For the next three and a half years he fought both of them.

6. EARLY 1942 IN AUSTRALIA

AT BRISBANE Pappy and the other Air Force personnel from the Philippines first realized that as far as substantial reinforcements were concerned, they were in a forgotten theatre of war. There was no expedition on the way to relieve MacArthur and only a handful of troops, badly in need of training and equipment, had even arrived in Australia. The news that Manila had fallen to the Japs on January 2, 1942, and the realization that his family was undoubtedly in their hands, contributed still further to Pappy's discouragement with the situation.

The only ray of hope was the arrival of twenty crated P-40 fighter planes which had arrived by ship in Brisbane Harbor that week, together with the news that another shipload was on the way. Without asking for instructions Pappy immediately organized a crew of Americans and Australians and started uncrating and assembling the airplanes. There were about twenty-five pilots of the old 17th Fighter Group available that had been flown out of the Philippines and Pappy mobilized them, too. Some of the parts of the planes were missing but with the help of local machine shops, by the middle of January they had been assembled, flight tested, guns had been installed, and they were ready to go.

On January 16 one flight of nine P-40's and another of eight left Brisbane for Darwin on orders from General Brereton. Everyone, including Pappy, thought their destination was the Philippines. As the pilots were far from being experienced in navigating, Pappy in his Beechcraft led one of the formations on the first leg to Townsville, seven hundred miles north of Brisbane with a stop at Rockhampton, about halfway, where they refuelled. Two Royal Australian Air Force Fairey Battle light bombers accompanied the other flight as far as Townsville. Two of the P-40's were wrecked landing at Rockhampton and were left behind for repair.

The next day Pappy's Beechcraft led the remaining fifteen fighters to the next stop at Cloncurry four hundred miles west of Townsville. Another P-40 was lost in landing at Cloncurry. Pappy led the remaining fourteen on the eighteenth to Daly Waters, another five hundred fifty miles to the northwest, got them refuelled, and late that same afternoon took them in to Batchelor Field at Darwin, a final flight of three hundred fifty miles.

Here the expedition remained for three days awaiting orders to move on while an impatient Pappy wondered what was delaying the war while checking every airplane to see that everything was in working order to continue the flight.

On January 21 General Brereton flew in from Brisbane and told them that they were not going to the Philippines but to Java. The next morning Pappy's Beechcraft led one flight of seven P-40's seven hundred fifty miles across the Java Sea to Waingapu on the island of Soemba, and then turned around and flew back to Darwin to lead the rest in to join the first flight on the twenty-third. There were now only thirteen P-40's in the picture, as one of the pilots had come down with dengue fever.

On January 24 and 25 Pappy got twelve of them to Soerabaja, Java, their destination. As soon as he could get gassed, he then flew back to Koepang on Timor Island to get a tire to replace one that had blown when the other P-40 had landed at Waingapu. On the return flight, Pappy must have been tired or sleepy for just before he hit the Soemba coast he almost rammed a four-engined Jap flying boat which came through a cloud directly ahead of him. However, before the astonished Japs could get a shot at him, Pappy dived under them, plunged into the cloud, and escaped. He landed at Waingapu, helped the P-40 pilot install the new tire, gassed, and checked over the Beechcraft, and after a few hours' sleep took off for Del Monte Field on Mindanao Island.

It never dawned on Pappy that he should ask anyone for instructions, and, besides, there was no one there to give him any. He knew that more fighter pilots were needed to fly the next shipload of P-40's soon to arrive in Brisbane. He also knew that there were several of them that had gotten out of Manila as far as Del Monte and he intended to ferry some of them to Australia. It also crossed his mind that he could perhaps get some information about his family even if he had to fly to Corregidor where MacArthur was. The first thing, however, was to get to Del Monte.

In order to avoid the Japs who had occupied Davao, the capital of Mindanao, Pappy gave that area a wide berth to the west. About ten miles beyond Zamboanga, just before dark, he had the bad luck to be spotted by a Jap float plane flying almost at treetop on his same level. Pappy had no guns, so he did the best he could to make himself a poor target, but the Jap gunners finally tagged him and shot him down. Through a miracle Pappy himself was not hit and survived the crash into the jungle with nothing more than a few scratches and bruises. He crawled out of the wreck, threw a lighted match into the gasoline leaking out of one of the tanks, and hid in the bushes watching the Jap plane circle the spot. It made three or four passes over the burning Beechcraft and then headed east toward Davao, evidently satisfied that there were no survivors.

By now it was getting dark. Pappy decided to get some sleep and not take a chance of getting thoroughly lost trying to make his way out at night. There had been no sign of the enemy when he passed over Zamboanga, so at first light he started walking in that direction. Late that afternoon he made the little flying field near the town just as Connelly landed with the third Beechcraft to pick up a B-17 tail wheel and a propeller from one of the bombers that had been wrecked there and abandoned back in December. With these spare parts there was some hope of getting the B-17 mat had been left at Del Monte back into the air. Connelly said one of the engines was still giving trouble, but if necessary the plane could be flown out on three engines. He also told Pappy that the Filipinos had told him that the Japs had picked up Polly and the four children and interned them at Santo Tomas University. That night he and Pappy flew back to Del Monte.

With Pappy's supervision and his own driving energy, the mechanics and pilots at Del Monte got the B-17 in flying condition during the next three days, and on the evening of February 1, with Pappy at the controls, the bomber took off and headed for Darwin.

There had been no opportunity to test flight the repaired bomber and one of the engines sounded pretty rough, but a total of twenty-two pilots and old-timer mechanics trusted Pappy enough to go with him. Connelly, with his Beechcraft, and six passengers followed.

Six hours later the B-17 landed at Darwin and was turned over to the 19th Bombardment Group. The rough engine had quit about three hundred miles off Australia but the remaining three had brought them in. Connelly arrived that afternoon after refuelling at Koepang and the next day he and Pappy with five fighter pilots took off for Brisbane.

Pappy had the reputation of being a human homing pigeon, and he was continually being called on to lead our other pilots who were not familiar with the geography of the southwest Pacific. Furthermore, no good maps were available, so a good flying guide such as Pappy came in pretty handy, but his methods of navigation were truly remarkable and formed the basis of many stories told by everyone who ever flew with him.

Major Tom Gerrity, an old fellow member of the 3rd Attack Group, says: "He never made any extensive preparations for a flight of any distance no matter where he was going. I recall one particular flight on which I accompanied him. This flight was from Brisbane, Australia, north to Townsville on the east coast en route to New Guinea. We were flying along at low altitude. Pappy seldom flew above five hundred feet. As we passed over the ground that was entirely unfamiliar to me I asked Pappy where we were and how he knew the direction to Townsville. At that point Pappy reached over to his navigation kit. As I looked into it when he opened it, I saw that it had no maps. However, it had a large bottle labelled 'Panther Juice.' Pappy pulled out the bottle, pretended to drink from it, then lifting his nose in the direction of flight and taking a long sniff, he said, 'Directly ahead of us is where we want to go.' Of course by this time I was somewhat doubtful of Pappy's navigation technique. I asked how this established the direction we should take. Pappy said, 'Well, some weeks ago I flew over this area and there was an old dead cow just ahead. I am following the smell.' In spite of such extraordinary navigation methods Pappy always got to his destination without any error. I never did see him refer to a map, yet on many flights with him I never found any error in his navigation. He apparently used that very old method of memorizing the terrain."

For the next month or so there is no official record of Pappy's actions, but he was too impatient to remain inactive. There is a story, however, that may or may not be true, but it sounds enough like him to be factual. According to the tale which I could never get him to confirm Pappy joined the Australians and flew a Boomerang fighter in the defence of Rabaul, the big port on the island of New Britain. The Boomerang was really nothing but a training plane with guns mounted on it and was no match for the Jap Zeros when they came in to cover the Jap troop landing. Most of the Boomerangs were shot down that day and among them was Pappy. He had managed to shoot down one Zero fighter when his engine was set on fire by a burst of machine-gun bullets from another enemy plane. Pappy took to his parachute and landed in the jungle about ten miles from Rabaul. For the next two weeks he made his way through the interior of the island and along the south coast until he reached the little settlement of Gasmata where he joined some other Australians and was evacuated to Australia in a flying boat.

During that two weeks' trip, according to the story, Pappy had lived on a diet that would probably have killed anyone else. For a day or two he had nothing but coconuts, but these soon made him sick. He ate jungle berries that he noticed the birds were eating and even grubs. The birds were eating these, too, and Pappy figured that if they could live on them so could he. One day he managed to kill a small boa constrictor. The meat didn't last very long but he got several good meals from the snake. Once he reached the coast he tried supplementing his diet with shellfish, but whether they were not the kind to be eaten or his stomach was too weak to handle them, he had to give them up as they made him sick. He learned a lot about jungle survival, but when he arrived in Gasmata he had dropped about twenty-five pounds.

While Pappy rarely told the actual facts of any of his exploits and adventures I am inclined to believe there was something to this story. Many times at mess he would test the stomachs of newly-arrived members of the squadron by describing the flavour of grubs, worms, and boa-constrictor meat. There were all kinds of bugs and beetles, too, he claimed, that would keep you alive if you just didn't eat the heads of some varieties or the tails of others. In a serious vein I've heard him instruct pilots how to live in the jungle in case they were forced down or had to parachute, and there were dozens of instances where his advice was followed and these youngsters survived and made their way back, some of them taking weeks to work . their way home through the New Guinea jungle.

In early April it was decided to put on a raid against Jap shipping in Davao and to the north around Manila itself. By this time some B-25 two-engined North American medium bombers had arrived in Australia which had range enough to make the flight from Darwin to Del Monte Field, which was still in our hands and had ample stocks of bombs and aviation fuel. Ten B-25's and 3 B-17's were to constitute the raiding force under the command of Brigadier General Ralph Royce. Here was Pappy's chance to get back to the Philippines again and carry on the two wars he was fighting. He promptly attached himself to the B-25 group as pilot and maintenance officer. Colonel "Big Jim" Davies, the commander, was so glad to get a man of Pappy's ability to maintain his airplanes in flying condition that he agreed that Captain Gunn should be one of the pilots on the raid.

There was one serious drawback to the success of the expedition that bothered Pappy. The B-25's had been sent to Australia without bomb sights. A few inquiries, however, brought forth the information that a Dutch squadron then in training in Canberra, the capital of Australia, had twelve B-25's equipped with bomb sights. Pappy decided to investigate the situation further.

With a sergeant named Evans who had attached himself to Gunn and had become almost a shadow, flying with him and working with him on every airplane that he had anything to do with, Pappy took a DC-2 transport and headed for Canberra. How he accomplished it I never found out, but the next day he was back at Brisbane with twelve brand-new Sperry bomb sights. He had enough to equip all ten B-25's and a couple of spares besides. When I got to Australia in July the Dutch were still complaining about the missing sights. I didn't know about what had happened so I told them they must have lost or mislaid them. By then we had enough bomb sights in stock, so I gave them enough to equip their airplanes, and the whole matter was forgotten.

The raid took place on April 12 when the three B-25's and the ten B-25's bombed the Jap shipping in Davao Harbor, continued on to Del Monte where they took on bombs and fuel and the following day struck at another shipping target at Cebu. Thanks to the "borrowed sights," the results were quite satisfactory. Returning to Del Monte, the expedition refuelled again, and loading on as many mechanics and pilots from that field as they could carry, flew back to Darwin. All planes returned safely and there were no casualties. Pappy had taken part in both bombings but had been unable to learn anything more than confirmation of the story that his family was still at Santo Tomas.

At Darwin Pappy received the sad news that Lieutenant Louis J. Connelly, one of his old Philippine Air Line pilots who had also been commissioned in the Army Air Force on the outbreak of the war, had been killed a few days before during a bombing raid on the Jap-held port of Lae on the north coast of New Guinea.

7. MY INTRODUCTION TO PAPPY

IT WAS August 5, 1942, when I first met Pappy Gunn at Charters Towers airdrome in Queensland, Australia, about thirty miles west of Townsville. I had reported to General Douglas MacArthur at his headquarters in Brisbane the week before to take over command of the Allied Air Forces then consisting of the United States Fifth Air Force, the Royal Australian Air Force, and the Netherlands East Indies Air Force, and I was inspecting my units for the first time.

The outfit at Charters Towers was the 3rd Attack Group, commanded by Colonel "Big Jim" Davies, consisting of the 8th, 13th, 89th, and 90th squadrons. The 8th had no airplanes at all, the 13th had a few A-24 Douglas dive bombers which didn't have range enough to reach any normal targets in New Guinea and were so slow that they had no business in this war. The 89th was equipped with about twelve B-25 North American Mitchell medium bombers which had only one 30-caliber front gun. Five of them were flyable. The rest were out of commission awaiting spare parts which as far as I could find out were still in the United States. The remaining squadron, the 90th, had sixteen A-20 Douglas light bombers, which had arrived in Australia with no guns and no bomb racks.

Pappy wasn't with Davies and the officers who met me when I arrived at Charters Towers, but over at the mess that noon, where I started my inspection by asking questions about the status of the group and their effectiveness for combat, it wasn't long before his name got into the conversation. It was quite evident that they all liked him, but more than anything else, they seemed to think that if there was anything about an airplane that needed fixing, Pappy could do it and that when he got through, it would be a better airplane. In addition, he was a genius at installing gun combinations and making them work better than anyone else. I also learned that he was a superb pilot on any type of aircraft big or little and that his idea of testing either an airplane or its gun installation was to try it out against the Japs. They told me some of the stories of his fabulous exploits but warned me that Pappy's stories while intensely interesting seldom dealt with his real achievements.

I asked Davies where Pappy was.

"Oh, you'll probably find him down at one of the hangars," said Jim. "He and another character, a sergeant named Evans, and a gang of mechanics are working over some A-20's. We've been sending coffee and sandwiches over to them for the last two days. Shall I send for Pappy?"

I said, "No, I don't want to interrupt his job that much, but after lunch I would like to inspect his show and meet this legend of yours."

It seemed that Pappy, who had been flying with any outfit that had anything to fly and free-lancing on his own since arriving in Australia from the Philippines the last of December 1941, had now settled down with the 3rd Attack Group as group engineering and maintenance officer and Colonel Davies was giving him free rein to get the outfit equipped for combat.

They told me one story about Pappy that was typical of many others. I never heard it from him and I forget who told it to me. I can't vouch for it, but it sounded enough like him so that I believe it. According to the tale, Pappy had been flying on a reconnaissance mission over the Coral Sea in a B-25 bomber looking for the Jap fleet which was supposed to be steaming south from the big enemy base at Rabaul.

Flying in and out of the low clouds and bad weather he had suddenly come upon a Jap cruiser. Instead of ducking back into the clouds and putting some distance between himself and the ship's anti-aircraft guns, Pappy decided to shoot up the enemy vessel with his front guns. He got away with two passes without getting hit, but on the third a shell fragment came through the cockpit and nailed his left hand to the side of the airplane. The jagged metal wrapped itself around his fingers and pierced the web between his thumb and forefinger so that he could not get it loose.

Pappy finished his run, flew back to the nearest air base in Australia, landed, and wanted to know if they had a good "veterinarian" who could cut him loose so that he could go back to work. The local Australian flight surgeon, assisted by a sergeant with a pair of sheet metal scissors, extricated Pappy's hand, sewed and bandaged it, and told Pappy he advised going to a hospital where it could be watched for infection. Pappy said "No," just fill up his gas tanks, and he would go to his home airdrome.

The Aussies gassed the airplane and Pappy took off. Instead of heading home he calmly headed out to sea, did another three-hour search flight over the Coral Sea, and just before dark landed at Charters Towers where the 3rd Attack Group was located.

Colonel Davies heard about the affair a few minutes later and in spite of Pappy's remonstrances had him flown to the army hospital in Sydney with instructions not to return until the hand was properly healed. It kept him out of the war for exactly one week. There was no infection. The cuts and lacerations did heal remarkably well. Pappy got a lot of good food and rest, both of which he needed badly, and was now ready to take on all comers.

On July 1 8, 1942, he had been made a major. No one, including Pappy, could understand why he had been promoted as it seemed to be common knowledge that he was about to be court-martialled instead of being given an advance in rank.

When the A-20's had arrived, he had let anyone who would listen to him know in definite and highly profane terms what he thought of everyone from Washington to Australia who had anything to do with sending airplanes to "his" outfit without guns or bomb racks to fight a war. Some of his listeners were staff inspectors. While they may have admired Pappy's command of language they didn't seem to appreciate his comments and so noted in their reports.

To add to his predicament, Pappy had by equally unorthodox methods managed to get hold of some 50-caliber machine guns, designed a package mount of four of them, and by rebuilding the entire nose of an A- 20 had installed them. He tested the installation himself by conducting a one-man raid at treetop level on a Jap airdrome on the north coast of New Guinea. He had done a good job, too. A couple of Jap airplanes that had just landed had gone up in smoke, a gasoline dump was left ablaze, and from all the explosions after Pappy had finished his strafing run, it looked as though he had also hit an ammunition dump.

He was now busy making more mounts to equip the rest of the A-20's in the squadron and designing a new bomb rack for them. The original bomb racks were supposed to be on a boat somewhere headed for Australia, but Pappy had never liked them anyhow and was making what he considered was a better rack. The funny thing about it was that he was right. It apparently hadn't occurred to him to ask permission of anyone to install an armament load that was nothing like the original one, or to bother about what anyone else thought about cutting the airplane all apart to make the new installations. Pappy thought it was a good idea. The whole 3rd Attack Group thought it was a good idea. That should be enough, even for some stupid "knuckle head" of an inspecting officer.

Colonel Davies took me over to Pappy's workshop, a tent hangar on the edge of the field. It was a hot day, but inside that canvas hangar it was stifling. All but one of the gang were stripped to the waist and working like sweating beavers under the direction of a tall, spare, blue-eyed, hawk-faced officer distinguished by the fact that he wore a mechanic's cap with a major's insignia pinned on it and an undershirt tucked into his khaki trousers.

Big Jim called him over and introduced him. "General," he said, "this is Major Gunn, our Engineering Officer who invents a new way to make it hard for the Japs every day."

We shook hands and walked over to the A-20 that the gang was working on. I said that I had heard about some of the armament innovations he had developed, and I wanted to know more about them. First, however, I wanted him to tell me about the job he was working on now.

Pappy wiped the sweat off his forehead, tilted his cap back, looked me over with a pair of steely blue eyes, grinned, and began to talk. He evidently had decided that I was intelligent enough to listen to him. I instinctively knew that I was being paid a compliment that had nothing to do with the two stars on the collar of my shirt.

In complete detail he described the gun installation, the method of feeding the ammunition, how the empty cartridges were ejected so that they wouldn't hit the tail surfaces on the way back, how the airplane flew, and what a fine job it was for getting rid of Jap airplanes if you could catch them on the ground. He knew what he was talking about, and I decided right then I had a find that I was going to put to work. I had a lot of ideas myself that I wanted someone like Pappy to play with. Furthermore, my inspections so far had shown that most of the airplanes I had inherited were out of commission and here was a real boss maintenance man made to order for me. I liked Pappy at first sight, and somehow I knew that he liked me and would break his neck carrying out my instructions. A lot of my ideas were unorthodox, too, but that would never bother Pappy.

As he talked you could almost see his enthusiasm and driving energy being communicated to his listeners. It was contagious. I could feel it myself. It was a nervous sort of energy almost fanatical. I couldn't put my finger on it, but I was sure of one thing. This was a useful man to have around. As we walked around the airplane looking over the installations he was making, I noticed that Pappy took care to introduce me to each member of his crew, always with some complimentary remark like,

"General, this is Corporal 'So and So.' He's a real fire-ball. He is getting so good, I believe we'll have to make a sergeant out of him soon." They liked him. You could see that right away.

Sergeant Evans, who Davies had told me was Pappy's crew chief, right-hand man, and adoring slave, was another slim, wiry lad about twenty-five or six who looked enough like his boss to be his brother. He didn't have much to say, but perhaps it was because Pappy talked so much he didn't have a chance. However, from the way his eyes followed Pappy around, you sensed that they were inseparable even if you hadn't already been told that the two made a team that should not be broken up.

As Davies and I walked back to the Group headquarters I told him he could have Pappy for another two weeks to finish the new gun and bomb-rack installations on his A-20's and then to send him to me at my headquarters in Brisbane as "special projects officer," and to have Sergeant Evans come along with him. Big Jim started to remonstrate, but I cut him short and told him to tell Pappy to train someone to take his place before he left Charters Towers.

On August 21 I returned to Brisbane from New Guinea and found Pappy waiting for me in my office. He said Colonel Davies had told him he was to report to me for some special duty. He just wanted to know what it was, as he was ready to go to work. Sergeant Evans was with him, nodding every time Pappy opened his mouth.

I told them to sit down and then described the first job I wanted them to work on. We had one hundred and seventy wrecked fighter planes out at Eagle Farms airdrome just west of Brisbane. They had been piled up there awaiting salvage but that wasn't what I intended being done with them as we had only seventy-five other fighters with the combat squadrons at the front and unless we got some more soon we weren't going to lick the Japs, who could throw three or four times that number at us on a single attack. Pappy was to reclaim the whole one hundred and seventy if possible. If he needed new parts to replace anything too badly damaged to repair, the tool shops and metalworkers of all Australia beginning at Brisbane were his to work with. I would okay any work order he wanted to put through. What I wanted were more fighter planes for New Guinea, and from the looks of things it would be a long time before I got any from the United States.

Pappy grinned happily and left with his "shadow" Sergeant Evans. How he ever did it I'll never know, but out of that pile of junk out at Eagle Farms we eventually got more than one hundred fighter planes that flew to

New Guinea and played a vital part in preventing the Japs from ousting us from that island and carrying out their original intention of invading Australia itself.

It wasn't long before I joined everyone else in the belief that Pappy could fix anything mechanical and make it work. One morning while shaving I dropped my electric razor. Pieces of the case and the mechanism of the razor were scattered all over the floor. I had gotten out of the habit of using any other kind and for the next couple of days I cut my face every time I shaved. Finally, in desperation, and also as a joke, I handed Pappy the pieces of the electric razor that I had saved, and asked him if he could fix it. He said, "Sure, General, I'll have it back for you tomorrow."

The next day he came into my office with the electric razor. It didn't look anything like the original, but it worked. The old plastic case had been repaired with part of the plastic dome of a gun turret from a wrecked airplane. The broken condenser had been replaced by another that weighed at least twice as much. Where it came from I don't know, but by the time it was hooked up with the rest of the razor, and the extra plastic added to cover it, I had a multi-coloured package much larger and much heavier than it had been before. It looked clumsy and was clumsy, and it made a noise like a lawn mower in action, but it worked.

The Australian current was all two hundred and twenty volts instead of the one hundred and ten volts all our American electrical appliances work on so that I had been using batteries to operate my razor. This was a nuisance, and the batteries lost their power after a few days and sometimes I would have trouble getting new ones. Pappy took care of this trouble also when he repaired and remodelled my electric razor. He hooked it up with a little transformer that allowed me to plug into any Australian outlet.

About two months later I got a new razor sent over from the United States by one of my friends, but from time to time I went back to using Pappy's version. Perhaps it was my imagination, but it seemed to me that it gave me a closer shave. I actually felt as though I had lost a close friend when it disappeared during one of my many moves more than a year later.

8. PAPPY'S FOLLY — THE SKIP-BOMBER

ABOUT THE middle of November 1942 I got another "brain storm" for Pappy to work on. We had started "skip bombing" with the B-17 heavy bombers but they didn't have enough forward gunfire to cover the low-altitude approach on the Jap vessels which were constantly loading more and more guns on their decks to combat our new tactics. I decided to remodel the B-25 medium bombers and make "commerce destroyers" out of them.

I sent word to Pappy at Brisbane to pull the bomb sight, the bombardier, and the one 30-caliber gun out of the nose of a B-25 and fill the place full of as many 50-caliber guns as he could squeeze in there, with five hundred rounds of ammunition per gun. I suggested that he also strap a couple more guns on each side of the fuselage and about three more underneath. If, when he had made the installation, the airplane would still fly and the guns would shoot without tearing the airplane apart, I figured I'd have a skip bomber that could overwhelm the deck defences of a Jap vessel as the plane came in for the kill with its bombs. With a "commerce destroyer" as effective as I believed this would be I'd be able to maintain an air blockade on the Japs anywhere within the radius of action of the airplane.

I had so much confidence in Pappy that I promptly put the whole scheme out of my mind for a couple of weeks while I was in New Guinea. At the end of that time I returned to Brisbane and went over to the hangar in which he had set up shop. He was really going to town on that B-25. He had a good-looking package of four 50-caliber guns and five hundred rounds of ammunition for each one tucked away in the nose where the bombardier and the bomb sight used to be. He was mounting a pair of guns on each side of the fuselage just under the pilot's window and three more underneath the fuselage.

The ammunition feed for the three underneath guns was a tough problem. It looked as though we might have to leave them off and be satisfied with eight forward-firing guns for a while. Pappy said that firing the guns on the ground at a target butt had knocked the rivets out of the fuselage skin, but he figured he could cure that trouble with longer blast tubes on the guns and by stiffening the gun mounts with steel plates. The airplane looked to me as though it might be getting a little nose heavy. I asked Pappy how about the centre of gravity. Pappy came right back with, "Oh, the C.G. Hell, General, we threw that away to save weight." I told him not to forget to do a little checking on the balance before he tried to take the plane off the ground and, if necessary, to put some lead in the tail to make up for the extra weight in the nose.

About a week or so later I dropped in to see Pappy again. He was just landing after a test flight in the remodelled B-25. He didn't come anywhere near getting his tail down as he came in. The plane was quite evidently nose heavy but Pappy was an excellent pilot. He taxied up to the line and got out sweating like a horse. I said, "Pappy, how does she handle?"

"Like a dream," Pappy replied, beaming all over. "And shoot?" he went on. "Say, General —"

I interrupted, "Pappy, don't you think about a hundred pounds of lead in the tail would make it easier for you to hold that nose up and keep you from sweating so much?"

"Oh, General," said Pappy, "I always sweat like that. I'm the nervous type. Still, it might be a good idea to make it a little easier for some of these kids who haven't had too much experience."

There was still a lot to be done to the B-25 to make the job right, but Pappy did it. He moved the side guns back to help out the balance and finally installed an extra two-hundred-gallon gasoline tank in the fuselage back of the wings which allowed him to leave off the lead in the tail and still balance the airplane besides giving us additional range to hit the Japs at greater distance than ever before. The business of knocking rivets out of the skins when firing the guns he finally cured by putting rubber pads between the guns and the fuselage skin. As a final touch and to take a little dig at the sceptics who didn't think loading all those guns on a B-25 made sense, the left side of the fuselage just below the pilot's window bore the words in eight-inch-high letters — PAPPY'S FOLLY. Alongside it was painted a two-gun cowboy with both guns drawn, a determined look on his face, and the message preceded by stars, crosses, and exclamation points — "And that's Plain English."

By the middle of December Pappy reported to me that he was ready to fly the job to Charters Towers and demonstrate it to the 3rd Attack Group. The gang had already heard about Pappy's latest creation and were looking forward to trying it out. I told him to demonstrate it, let the other pilots play with it, and if it worked out all right, to get ready to modify twelve more B-25's so that we could give a real test against the first Jap ship convoy that came within reach.

The next day Pappy took off from Charters Towers with five other B-25's following him, to watch the result of all these guns firing at once on a low-altitude simulated attack. The demonstration was a huge success except that an Australian cow wandered into the line of fire and the farmer entered a complaint when he discovered the corpse a few days later. By this time Pappy had gone back to Brisbane. The 3rd Attack Group swore that they had had nothing to do with killing the cow and while still not satisfied the farmer left. I didn't hear about it for more than a month but I told the gang to find out who the owner was and had our finance officer pay the bill, charging it up to the war effort.

After demonstrating his remodelled B-25 at Charters Towers Pappy, with Sergeant Evans in the co-pilot's seat, took off for New Guinea to show the airplane to the gang up there. A combination of prickly heat and one or more kinds of jungle itch was bothering him at the time and the equatorial heat as he got north didn't help it any. In order to get comfortable he took off his clothes until he had nothing on but his shoes and socks, his cap, and something that resembled an aborigine's G-string. His trousers, shirt, and underclothes were thrown into the bomb bay to get them out of the pilot's cockpit where they might interfere with the controls.

Arriving at Seven Mile strip at Port Moresby, Pappy followed his customary procedure of "buzzing" the area at low altitude, to let everyone know he was there, before landing. He taxied up to the line where an appreciative crowd was waiting for him. Perhaps he would have a story for them.

About a month before we had flown a half-dozen Red Cross girls up to New Guinea to run a recreation hut and meet the airplanes coming back from missions with coffee and sandwiches. This last job was a popular one with the girls, who liked to load their refreshments on a jeep and drive to the field to see the planes come in.

Pappy didn't know it, and probably Sergeant Evans hadn't realized it, but when Pappy had finally decided to land and called on the sergeant for "wheels down," Evans had by mistake opened the bomb-bay doors. Quickly realizing his mistake, he shut them and then lowered the landing gear. In the meantime Pappy's clothes were gently settling into the jungle a good mile away from the field.

The sergeant got out to put the chocks in front of the wheels and tie down the airplane. Pappy looked out the window, saw the Red Cross girl approaching the airplane, and reached for his clothes. No clothes. He let out a yell for Evans, who stuck his head in the plane to see what was the matter.

"Go get a pair of pants and a shirt and hurry up," he whispered, "and keep that damn girl away from here. Tell her I don't like coffee and I don't like women. Tell her I'm — tell her anything, but keep her away. Do you hear me, you knuckle head?"

The sergeant nodded and hurried toward the operations hut. On the way he stopped and said something to the Red Cross girl, who looked puzzled and then drove her jeep up to the airplane. Evidently she hadn't understood Evans or thought Pappy was sick. Pappy saw her coming, shut the hatch, and held onto the handle yelling to her to go away and leave him alone. When she started to climb up on a landing wheel to look in the window Pappy was desperate but equal to the occasion.

"Get the hell away from there!" he roared. "I'm going to start up the engines. Do you want your fool head knocked off by a prop?"

The girl hastily retreated far enough to be out of danger and sat there in the jeep still puzzled but evidently determined to find out what all the commotion was about.

In the meantime Sergeant Evans was having no luck. By this time everyone except the Red Cross worker knew of Pappy's predicament and they were going to let him sweat it out. No one had any spare clothes and didn't think there were any in New Guinea. Pappy was taking the thing so seriously that now they were going to have some fun at his expense.

Evans came back and reported the situation. Pappy told him to pull the chock blocks away from the wheels and started up the engines. The gang now realized that Pappy was capable of taking off to get himself out of the jam. Miraculously a pair of trousers and a shirt appeared and were waved in front of the airplane. Someone talked to the Red Cross girl, who hurriedly drove away, and Pappy, thoroughly mad but at least clothed, strode off toward the mess hall telling Sergeant Evans to bed down the airplane and join him as soon as he was through. No one dared to ask him for any stories that evening, and Pappy didn't volunteer any.

9. PAPPY VISITS THE UNITED STATES

ON MARCH 1, 1943, a Jap convoy of about twenty ships, including destroyer escorts, left Rabaul, their big base on the east end of New Britain, for Lae, a port on the north coast of New Guinea. The purpose was to reinforce the Jap garrison there and bring them some much-needed supplies of food and ammunition.

We threw our whole air strength of more than one hundred and thirty bombers and fighters against the convoy and practically annihilated it. All the cargo and troop ships were sunk together with all the destroyer escorts except two that, although badly damaged, managed to get back to Rabaul. In addition, the Japs lost sixty fighter planes which were covering their fleet. We lost one bomber and three fighters. The engagement, known later as the Battle of the Bismarck Sea, was opened by twelve of Pappy Gunn's modified B-25 bombers which in their initial combat mission skip bombed and sank four cargo vessels and two destroyers in the first fifteen minutes of the attack. All twelve of the planes returned to their home airdrome.

The pilots of the 3rd Attack Group, to which the B-25's had been assigned, had become so enthusiastic about them that they wouldn't let Pappy fly one in the battle. Pappy fumed and protested but finally had to be contented with acting as a co-pilot on one of the bigger B-17 bombers. If he hadn't at least seen the big brawl, I believe he would have crossed the whole Air Force off his visiting list. As it was, every time the Bismarck Sea Battle was mentioned for the next six months he complained to me about the injustice he had suffered.

Two days later General MacArthur sent me to Washington to discuss our future plans and immediate need of reinforcements with the Joint Chiefs of Staff. Everyone all the way up to President Roosevelt wanted to know the details of the battle. I particularly emphasized the work of the B-25's and the remodelling job Pappy had done, so that soon his name was known all over the Air Force.

Back in January I had sent General "Hap" Arnold, chief of Army Air Forces, a set of drawings showing the modifications Pappy had made, and asked that in the future to have the B-25's built this way at J. H. "Dutch" Kindelberger's North American Aircraft plant in Los Angeles.

While in Washington one day, Hap asked me to come into his office for a conference with a battery of engineering experts from the Air Force Materiel Division at Dayton, Ohio. For about an hour they explained to me that the idea was impractical. They insisted that the balance would be all messed up, the airplane would be too heavy, would not fly properly, and so on.

I listened as patiently as I could and then explained that twelve B-25's fixed up in this manner had played a rather important part in the Bismarck Sea Battle and that I was now remodelling sixty more in Australia. Arnold glared at his "experts" and practically ran them out of the office. He then turned to me and said, "I want that man Pappy Gunn transferred to Dayton to teach my engineers something."

I offered to lend Pappy to him for a month to go to the North American plant but objected strenuously to losing my uninhibited experimenter. I said I needed him badly myself and, in addition, if Pappy went to Dayton he would either ruin Hap's engineers or they would civilize him and ruin him for my purposes. General Arnold laughed and said, "Okay, let me have him for a month or six weeks and I'll send him back to you. Get a wire off to him right away and we will start getting your B-25's remodelled his way as soon as he arrives."

Pappy arrived in San Francisco about the first of April 1943. There he got orders to go to Wright Field just outside of Dayton, Ohio, for a few days. General Arnold wanted the officers of the Engineering Division there to be exposed to someone with war experience. I don't think he realized what he was letting them in for.

Before leaving San Francisco Pappy called his sister Jewell Owen, living at Texarkana, Texas, to find out the family news. Jewell took the train for Dayton that night and for several days thoroughly enjoyed herself as Pappy showed her over the big Air Force station and regaled her with his stories of the Pacific war.

How much the Wright Field people enjoyed Pappy's stay is hard to tell but they all agreed afterward that it had been an interesting week and that he had brought home to them quite vividly the differences between fighting the war in New Guinea and in Dayton, Ohio.

The orderly, systematic routine of a large zone of the interior installation such as Wright Field did not appeal to Pappy at all and he didn't hesitate to tell everyone there that it did not have the proper tone of activity that he was accustomed to. The endless stream of papers that had to be filled out before, during, and after a job was done brought the wrathful comment that "back in New Guinea we don't care if you can read or write if you can make a bomb rack work or get a gun to shoot."

Actually, however, Pappy accomplished a good deal during the visit explaining the changes in equipment that we were making in the Southwest and helping to prepare the instructions that went to the aircraft industry to incorporate them in aircraft destined to come our way. Of course they first had to be told what we wanted, but in the long run it was much better for these modifications to be made at the factory in the United States than under some palm tree in New Guinea, Pappy Gunn told them.

During his visit to Wright Field Pappy and Jewell stayed with Colonel Tom Gerrity and his wife, Marge. Gerrity had come out of the Philippines with Pappy and they both had been members of the 3rd Attack Group in Australia. Shortly after I had annexed Gunn to my own staff Tom had gone back home and after getting his malaria taken care of had been assigned to Wright Field which was the Air Force headquarters for development, engineering, testing, purchase, and supply of all aviation equipment.

Marge still laughs every time anyone mentions Pappy Gunn. She enjoyed every minute of the stay, listened with proper appreciation to his stories, and became quite fond of his sister Jewell. Marge says: "Mrs. Owen was sweet, lovely, white-haired, and motherly looking — very unlike what he had expected Pappy's sister to be. She was naturally overjoyed at the prospect of seeing Paul, as she called him, after twelve years. We spent several quiet family-type evenings at home to give her an opportunity to chat and visit with Pappy while she sat and crocheted.

"During his stay with us, a friend of mine, a Mrs. Larson, visited us from Chicago. In hopes of showing Pappy a few of the bright lights around Dayton we decided to make a foursome and go into town to one of the hotels for dinner and some dancing. Pappy had his uniform on all the way to his cowboy boots, so we proceeded into town for a gay evening. After dinner Pappy entered into the festivities with enthusiasm. He asked my friend to dance and as they stepped on the dance floor, she made some apology for her style of dancing. Pappy said, 'Oh, don't worry, I dance in seven different languages.' After observing him on the dance floor we quite agreed. His dancing seemed to be a combination of the polka and the jig, with a little sprinkling of South Sea hula and the occasional stamping of the New Guinea natives. He created quite a sensation and enjoyed himself hugely.

"Although Pappy had a seemingly gruff manner about him we were most impressed to learn of his extreme devotion to his family. After returning from the hotel that night we went upstairs to tuck our young son into bed and Pappy tagged along. As I left the room, I noticed tears in his eyes. His remark was, 'This reminds me of the evenings when my wife and I have been out having fun and then coming home and tucking our children in bed. You know all four of the children and Mrs. Gunn are in Santo Tomas and I'm going to get them out if it is the last thing I ever do.'

"I had my own experience seeing Pappy accomplish almost anything working with metals. One evening I had left my coffeepot on the stove and the bottom burned out completely. I was ready to throw it away, when Pappy came in and said, 'Oh, don't throw it away. I'll fix it for you.' Since those things were hard to get during the war years I was happy to let him try. He did repair it, put a new bottom on it, and returned it to me with the remark, 'This was not half as hard to do as putting all those guns on the B-25.'"

After a week or so at Wright Field Pappy got an airplane assigned to him for the trip to the North American factory at Los Angeles, and without worrying about a trifle like permission for Jewell to accompany him, loaded her aboard and flew to Little Rock, Arkansas. All his relatives met him at the airport, where Pappy got the welcome of a returned hero and becomingly enjoyed it. Has Owen, his brother-in-law, then drove him to Texarkana, where Pappy got another welcome. Two days later he took off for Los Angeles and reported in to "Dutch" Kindelberger.

10. PAPPY IN HOLLYWOOD

FOR THE next three weeks Pappy practically lived in the factory, working day and night with the engineers and aircraft workers at the North American plant. He not only showed them what he wanted done to the B-25, but demonstrated the job by doing it himself. By the time the modification was done, it was a real improvement on his original job. The B-25 now had six 50-caliber guns in the nose instead of four and still had a pair mounted on each side of the fuselage.

Some of the factory crowd decided about this time that Pappy was getting tired and needed a little relaxation and change of scenery. A week-end party was arranged for him at one of the Hollywood estates with a swimming pool attached, and a bevy of starlets added further to enhance the scenery. Pappy wasted no time in giving the party a picture of what the war in the Pacific was like.

One of those present described the scene to me. Pappy was sitting on the edge of the pool telling his stories with a couple of starlets on each side of him and another lying on the diving board. The girls and other guests grouped around were listening wide-eyed as Pappy reeled off his lurid tales. He had a good audience that hadn't heard them before and he was enjoying himself. Approximately as Pappy told it here is the story that finally broke up the party.

"It was during the campaign to capture Buna on the north coast of New Guinea last December. The advance of the Australians was held up by a big Jap fortified bunker of logs covered over with four or five feet of dirt. Inside were a couple of pieces of artillery, some mortars and machine guns and a garrison of about fifty Japs. Three or four hundred other Japs were in trenches on each side of the bunker.

"I flew over and looked at it from the air and then went back and told the general I would take it out for him. He said go ahead and that the Australians would rush forward as I blew it up. I said, 'Okay, how about tomorrow morning at ten o'clock?' We set that time and I went to work to fix up my plane.

"It was too dangerous a job to risk other lives on, so I decided to do it alone. I fixed the bomb release so I could work it from the pilot's seat and hooked up the machine guns the same way. I got my bombs and gasoline loaded on and by this time it was about nine o'clock and I had to take off to keep my date with the Australians.

"I came in low just on the treetops, shooting all ten of my forward guns, and slid my load of bombs right in through the door of that bunker. The Japs filled the air with bullets and shells which tore my plane almost to ribbons, but she still flew. As I let go the bombs, I pulled up steep to get out of there and just then one of their shells cut the whole tail off the ship. Luckily I had gotten up about three hundred feet so I just bailed out and pulled my parachute rip cord. Just then my bombs, which had delay fuses in them, went off. The blast and a fairly strong wind that was blowing away from the Japs carried me over toward the Australian position and when I landed, it was among them as they rushed forward to capitalize on my destruction of the bunker which had gone up like a volcano, spouting fire, smoke, logs, dirt and Japs. I guess I must have hit a pile of ammunition the way things happened when those bombs went off.

"Well, there I am, right in the middle of a charge. I pull my pistol from my shoulder holster and start moving along with the Aussies. Just then one of 'em falls and I grab his bayoneted rifle and keep on going. It's funny the way things run through your mind at times like this, but I remembered one of the 3rd Group gang had said he wished he could get one of those Japanese samurai swords for a souvenir. I decided this was a good chance to get one for him. But only officers wore swords, and believe it or not I had to kill six Japs before I got one with rank enough to wear a sword and then kill two more who tried to take it away from me.

"By this time I am about to collapse from hunger, thirst, and fatigue. You see I had worked all the afternoon before and all night, too, without stopping to eat or sleep or even get a drink of water. As a matter of fact, I had been too busy even to eat breakfast. Now I was about to keel over, but I just had to keep going somehow, although things were beginning to blur and I guess I hardly knew what I was doing. Then something happened that snapped me out of it, but I don't believe I'd better tell you that part of it — it's kinda rough." He hesitated.

A chorus broke out of, "Go ahead, tell us, never mind how rough it is, we want to hear the rest of the story." Pappy had baited the trap. Now if they fell into it it would be their own fault. He shrugged his shoulders, sighed, as though reluctant to give in to them, and resumed his story.

"Yes," he went on, "I was getting weaker and thirstier all the time I was killing these Japs. The last one, the eighth, took all the strength I had left to shove the bayonet in him. He fell forward directly at me and there right in front of my eyes was a nice fat round shoulder. I just couldn't resist the temptation. I grabbed that shoulder with both my hands and sank my teeth in it. That Jap's blood restored my strength and kept me going ...

At this point the girl who had been lying on her tummy on the diving board gasped, fainted, and rolled off into the pool. The starlets on each side of Pappy were collapsing into the water, their escorts were diving in to rescue them, and with all this commotion the story stopped. How much further it would have run nobody knows. Pappy just sat there grinning and quite evidently enjoying himself. This was better than any applause his New Guinea audiences had ever given him. He knew that he had done a good job when the party broke up a few minutes later. No one asked for any more stories. In fact, a lot of the guests left without even saying good-by to either their host or his guest.

There actually was a big Jap bunker bombed and destroyed during the Buna campaign and Pappy was on the flight with the squadron that did the job. That was more than enough background for him around which to weave one of his fantasies. I've often thought what a pity it was that Pappy didn't know about flying saucers in those days.

That Sunday evening Pappy was back in the factory working harder than ever. The weekend and the tribute to his powers as a raconteur had acted like a tonic.

About the first of May up at my headquarters in New Guinea I heard a lot of commotion outside. I looked out the door and there was Pappy just getting out of a jeep surrounded by an admiring crowd slapping him on the back and welcoming home their beloved storyteller. I was just as glad to see him as the rest. I liked those stories, too. Besides, I had some more ideas I wanted him to work on.

11. THE TALE OF A SHIRT

ONE DAY in May, just after his return from the North American factory in Los Angeles, Pappy came into my office in Brisbane and without any preliminaries stated his case.

"General," he said, "how do I get a pair of wings like those?" He pointed to the pilot's insignia I was wearing.

"Oh, go over to the post exchange and buy a pair," I replied.

"That won't do me any good," said Pappy. "I haven't any authority to wear them. I haven't any pilot's rating. In fact, I shouldn't be flying a plane for you."

I knew that he had flown every type of airplane we had and had been on probably a hundred combat missions by that time.

"How the devil do you happen to be flying anyhow? Where did you learn to fly in the first place? Don't you even draw flying pay?" I asked.

"Well," said Pappy, "I put in twenty years with the Navy and got a pilot's rating from them back in 1925. When the Japs started the war I was running the Philippine Air Lines and General Brereton mobilized me and my airplanes. I was sworn in as a captain in the Air Force and told to organize an air transport service. He said he'd send the papers in to Washington and legalize me as a pilot but I guess those papers must have gotten lost as I've never heard anything more about it. I'd sure like to be a legal pilot just the same. No," he added, as an afterthought. "I've never drawn any flying pay. The finance officer said he had no authority to pay it to me."

I promised Pappy I'd take care of it and he left the office. I immediately wired General Arnold and asked him to give Major Paul I. Gunn the rating of airplane pilot in the Air Force effective December 7, 1941. The message was evidently answered by some staff officer for the general, or at least that was what I assumed when it said to send Major Gunn back to the United States where he would be given flying training. If at the end of about nine months he had qualified, he would be sent back to me unless he asked for some other assignment.

As soon as I had calmed down I sent a personal wire to Arnold marked "Eyes Only," which told Hap the story of Pappy's life, suggesting a suitable disposition of the staff officer who had sent me the answer to my original wire, and inasmuch as I believed that Major Gunn knew more about flying than any instructor he had in the United States, I was again asking that Pappy be rated an Air Force pilot.

Hap wired back rating Pappy as a pilot effective December 7, 1941. I sent for him and pinned on his wings. He thanked me and left for the finance office where he drew about four thousand dollars in back flying pay. In a few minutes he was back in my office asking if he could take a trip to New Guinea. He had all his money in large-denomination Australian bills secured in his shirt pocket with a big safety pin. I said, "Sure, Pappy, go ahead, but what are you going to do with all that money?"

Pappy grinned. "General, by tomorrow I'll be a millionaire. I'm going to break up every crap game in New Guinea." I let him go.

He got aboard as co-pilot on a B-25 bomber being delivered to New Guinea, telling everyone about what he was going to do with that big stake to back up his judgment as to the behaviour of a pair of galloping dice.

Halfway across the Coral Sea, between Townsville and New Guinea, the cockpit became hotter and hotter under the equatorial sun. Pappy took off his shirt and draped it across his lap. It was still too hot and rather stuffy from the big cigar he was smoking, so to get better ventilation, Pappy reached for the handle on the side window. Anyone else would have slowly slid the window back an inch or two and gotten all the air necessary, but Pappy was a creature of impulse who never did things by half. With a quick jerk he slid the window back its full two feet of travel. Before he could grab it, the money-laden shirt was sucked off his lap and into the blue. He looked back to see if it had hung up on the tail surfaces. It hadn't.

He reached for the control wheel which the pilot gave him without question. Pappy then circled around for about ten minutes looking down on the surface of the ocean to see if he could spot that shirt. If he could locate it, maybe he could call a ship on the radio and have them home on the B-25 and pick up his money. He didn't find the shirt and anyway there was no ship clear to the horizon in any direction. Pappy finally straightened the airplane out, put it on course for Port Moresby, and turned the controls back to the pilot.

He settled back in his seat, took a few more puffs on his cigar, looked at it reflectively for a while, then pitched it overboard. When the air had cleared, he carefully shut the window, turned to the pilot, and in a resigned voice remarked, "Well, I guess it's come easy — go easy."

We all figured that as far as Pappy was concerned the incident was closed, but as time went on I began to hear variations of the "lost-shirt" story. The amounts of money varied and sometimes it was Pappy's pants that were lost instead of the shirt. The flight varied, of course, to fit the locality of the audience which gathered around wherever he arrived. I heard the story at Darwin where Pappy had landed and departed a few days before I got there. Down in Melbourne the incident was supposed to have taken place on one of Pappy's flights from Brisbane south. It had such a good background that Pappy couldn't resist adding it to his collection. Eventually, however, the stories stopped. The rumour that went around Air Force circles was that Pappy's Sergeant Evans had caught the fever and was beginning to tell the yarn with himself in the role of the hero who hauled Pappy back in the cockpit when he tried to go out the window after his money. This same rumour said that after bawling the daylights out of Evans for telling such a lie, Pappy decided the story had had sufficient play and should be dropped. By this time he probably had several good substitutes and no longer needed it.

12. PROMOTION PARTY

ON MAY 10, 1943, I signed an order promoting Major Paul I. Gunn to the rank of lieutenant colonel. There were several others on the list including one of his special pals, John "Jock" Henebry who commanded the famous skip-bombing outfit, the 3rd Attack Group. It was Pappy's favourite unit and the one he had led when he first demonstrated the 7 5 - millimetre gun mounted in the nose of a B-25 bomber during the attack on two Jap destroyers off the north coast of New Britain.

We were all up at Port Moresby, in New Guinea, at the time. Pappy and Jock wanted me to pin the silver leaves of their new insignia on them and Colonel "Big Jim" Davies, who had recently been made head of the 5th Bomber Command, threw a party at his headquarters mess for the occasion. It was a good party. I pinned the silver leaves on my two new lieutenant colonels and about midnight left for my own headquarters.

The next day when I asked for Pappy I found that he had taken off during the night for Archer Field just outside of Brisbane, Australia, where he had his "experimental" workshop. I had told him I wanted some racks designed to carry rockets on the wings of our fighter and light bomber aircraft. I had heard that they were producing the rockets back home and I wanted to be ready for them when I got them. I didn't think it strange that Pappy had left. In fact, I had long since quit thinking anything he did was strange. He always had a good reason for everything.

I returned to Australia a few days later and learned that Pappy had been to the hospital to get X-rayed and that he was wearing several layers of adhesive tape around his ribs.

Pappy never told me anything about it but I gradually pieced the story together.

Shortly after I had left Big Jim Davies' promotion party Pappy had decided to go to bed in spite of repeated invitations to stay up and tell some more stories. The gang waited until the snores from Pappy's room indicated that he was asleep. Someone, I didn't think it was necessary to investigate too far, got a half stick of dynamite, set the fuse to delay about five minutes, and placed it outside the hut opposite where Pappy was sleeping. The gang lit the fuse, hurried into their beds, pretending to be asleep, and waited for the explosion. It came on time. Possibly from the blast but probably more from being suddenly awakened and startled by the roar of the explosion, Pappy, tangled in his blankets and mixed up with the cot on top of him, crashed up against the thin cardboard wall of his room and broke through into another section of the hut where several of the gang were pretending to be asleep. When no longer able to hold back they laughed at Pappy trying to untangle himself, and the jig was up. Pappy still didn't like jokes if he was the victim.

Without saying a word he dressed, stalked out of the hut, and taking Big Jim's jeep, headed for the airdrome and took off for Australia.

The next day he felt so sore in the lower part of his chest that he went to the hospital to get checked up. The X rays showed a small crack in one of his ribs. The doctor taped his chest and told him not to worry about it. It would be healed up in a week, and then he could take off the adhesive.

Months later it became a good story according to the reports that drifted back to me. By this time it was a whole stick of dynamite that had exploded under the middle of his cot and had blown him through the wall into the next room breaking several of his ribs and causing him difficulty in breathing for more than a month.

I doubt whether the difficulty in breathing had anything to do with it but it was nearly a month before Pappy got back to New Guinea to see any of the gang that had been at Big Jim's when the big blowoff occurred. Of course he was busy inventing some rocket racks for me during that time, but I suspect his pride was hurt too. The worst of it was that we didn't hear any stories during that time. Everyone, including the culprits, decided that they had lost more than they had gained, in spite of the fact that they had managed the rare feat of putting one over on Pappy. It wasn't an easy thing to do and Pappy didn't seem to mind them trying, but this last one had been a little too rough.

On his return to Australia after working in the North American Aviation Corporation's plant in Los Angeles on armament modifications in their B-25 bomber, Pappy hunted up Jack Fox, the local representative of that company in Brisbane and told him about the changes he had worked out in the factory and some more ideas he had thought of during the flight from Los Angeles back to Australia. While they were waiting for the delivery from the United States of the modified B-25's, they worked together on changes to be made in the airplanes already in the Southwest Pacific theatre.

Just for fun the two began to refer to themselves as the South American Aviation Corporation and designed a letterhead on which they wrote letters back to North American and to the Air Force Engineering Division at Dayton, Ohio, trying to expedite the changes on the B-25 and delivery of the modified airplanes to the Pacific.

By this time Pappy and Jack Fox had acquired the reputation of being capable of being willing and able to install anything on a B-25 from a tank to a battery of 16-inch coast-defence guns. The inevitable cartoons began to appear. The best of the lot was a drawing bearing the title "Pappy Gunn's Future B-25 Project" to be produced by the South American Aviation Corporation. The drawing showed what resembled a B-25, except that it had four engines instead of two, a huge caterpillar tractor in place of the landing gear, and with fore-and-aft turrets of artillery of about the calibre normally installed in battleships. In addition to a sort of ship's bridge for the commander's station, the whole fantastic design was topped by something that looked like a lighthouse.

The strange thing about it was that Pappy was as proud of the idea as if he had drawn it himself. He displayed the drawing so often and made so many sales talks for its features that some of his listeners were not sure whether he was really going to build the job or was playing another of his jokes on his unsuspecting but always-appreciative audience.

About this time we got some news of Pappy's family. We were in constant radio communication with the Philippine guerrillas who were holding out in spots all over the Islands. The Japs controlled the cities and the main roads, but in spite of constant raids and fairly large-scale punitive expeditions they never were able to dislodge the guerrillas from the mountainous jungle-covered interior. The guerrillas mingled with the native population in spite of all Jap efforts, even entering the cities and reporting to us in Australia and New Guinea by coded radio messages any information they could gather. Through these sources we learned that Polly and the four children were still alive and still interned in Santo Tomas University.

I asked Pappy if he didn't want me to get a message back to his wife saying that he was well or something. He begged me please to forget all about the idea. He said that if by any chance the Japs caught the messenger, they would torture the information out of him before they shot him as a spy. He explained to me that he had told Polly to tell the Japs that her husband had been flying for the Americans at the start of the war but that he had been killed in an accident soon after. If the Japs learned that Polly had been lying to them, they would take it out on her and the children. I promised him that I would not send Polly any message and would caution the Signal Corps crowd never to mention Pappy's name in any radio message to the Philippines.

I think it was at this time that I first realized what was back of Pappy's driving energy, his seeming recklessness, and his outrageous stories.

It was all part of a mask to cover up his deep concern for his family and keep his mind from dwelling constantly on the fact that they were at the mercy of an enemy who knew no mercy and to whom life was the cheapest commodity on earth.

The Air Force fliers and mechanics in New Guinea, eight thousand miles from home, were living in a terrible climate, eating poor food, suffering from malaria, dengue fever, and all the itches the jungle inflicts. They had no place to go for recreation and sometimes went for months without hearing from home. Pappy's stories were wonderful morale builders. They were real entertainment, particularly when everyone knew that his actual exploits, which he never mentioned, were truly heroic. I don't think that at the time many of them realized what motivated Pappy's telling of his yarns, but the fact remains that they were a real contribution to our war effort in the Southwest Pacific and probably as important in the final analysis as his actual achievements. We owed a lot to Pappy Gunn.

13. PRACTICAL JOKE

THE 3rd ATTACK GROUP liked to play practical jokes on Pappy. They seldom succeeded in putting them across, but that only increased the incentive. It became a kind of contest. Besides they liked him. You don't play practical jokes on people you dislike — you ignore them. You couldn't ignore Pappy. He had too much personality for that, he was a likable character, and he also enjoyed the contest, especially when he outwitted his opponents and turned their defeat into a background for another story. Perhaps that was the main reason for the game. At the same time, being a normal human being, Pappy didn't like it when he lost. He seldom thought of retaliatory measures, but for a few days after each of their rare "victories," the jokesters were made to realize that Pappy was at least displeased.

The promotion party episode, however, went a little too far. Pappy didn't like it at all. He felt that his dignity had suffered a setback, and for the first and only time that I remember, he began to entertain an idea of a counterattack. This would have to be a foolproof scheme guaranteed to bring retribution on the heads of the three ringleaders in that last practical joke and restore his prestige.

Pappy was billeted along with a lot of other captains, majors, and lieutenant colonels, all members of the Air Force and Army Headquarters staffs, in one of Brisbane's smaller hotels that had been taken over by the military. He got along with everyone except a certain quartermaster major who had a much larger and better room than Pappy. The friction had nothing to do with the fact that Pappy was now a lieutenant colonel. He just didn't like the major for some reason. I never did find out why. Pappy now decided that the major was to play an important part in his plot. Their rooms were on the same floor and across the hall from each other.

After a certain number of combat missions in New Guinea we allowed the airplane crews a week in Australia to relax, forget about the war, and most important of all, to get some of the country's excellent food under their belts. The ration situation in New Guinea was never very good, and the hot, steaming, jungle weather didn't help the appetite any.

The three practical jokers who were the reason for Pappy's plot always managed to take their leave together, and they liked Brisbane better than any other Australian city. The quartermaster major made frequent trips from Brisbane to Sydney, where the Army Service of Supply headquarters was located, and was generally gone for three or four days at a time. Pappy began to cultivate him and succeeded so well that it wasn't long before he found out that on Monday the following week, the major would be making one of his trips to Sydney and would be gone for three days. Pappy had already managed to get a duplicate key to his neighbour's room.

Pappy headed for New Guinea, greeted everyone in the 3rd Attack Group as though nothing had happened, and during the course of the evening, developed the details of his plot. Everyone knew that hotel rooms in Brisbane were almost impossible to get. Visitors from New Guinea generally stayed at Archer Field, about twenty miles from town, in the barracks. There was not only the question of transportation to and from the delights of Brisbane, but the barracks accommodations were not to be compared to those of a city hotel.

Pappy explained to the three objects of his scheme that if they happened to take a leave the following week they would really be sitting pretty. He was going to be away from Brisbane himself during that time so that one of them could have his room and a friend of his across the hall was going to be gone all that week. His friend's room had two beds, which would take care of the other two. Pappy produced the keys to the two rooms and said that beginning Monday afternoon, they could start having fun. This was Saturday. The delighted trio, who had been eligible for a leave for some time, made their arrangements with the squadron commander and Monday morning got a ride on one of our cargo supply planes returning to Brisbane.

Pappy remained in New Guinea to wait for results. About Wednesday or Thursday the quartermaster major would be coming back from Sydney. He was a pompous, hot-tempered, fat little man who was certainly going to be annoyed to find two aviators in his room. Pappy speculated to himself about what would happen. They would certainly have some explaining to do. Perhaps they would be so chagrined that they would slink out of the hotel apologetically and head back for New Guinea to avoid being kidded by the rest of the aviators in Brisbane. Of course, that would mess up their leave, but it would serve them right.

On the other hand, all three of those rascals were tough guys in their own right. Maybe, whether or not they had been having a few drinks, they would throw that quartermaster major out of the place. Then he would complain to the hotel manager or even to the military police. No matter how he figured it, Pappy could see nothing but discomfort and confusion for the three lads and satisfaction for himself.

By Friday, however, they hadn't returned and Pappy began to worry. Remorse set in. Suppose that they had slugged the major, been arrested, and were now due for a court-martial. He didn't want to see them get in trouble. He had just wanted to embarrass them. After all, he liked this bunch of guys. He already wished that he had never started this crazy scheme.

In the meantime, the three aviators were thoroughly enjoying themselves in Brisbane. For a wartime city it was a pretty good place to spend a few days' leave. They had done an excellent job forgetting about the war until Saturday arrived with its reminder that the next morning they had three seats on a cargo plane for New Guinea.

The occasion called for a farewell party to celebrate. As there was more room in the quartermaster major's quarters than in Pappy's for a party, they decided to hold it there. The major had been detained for several extra days in Sydney, so he had not returned to carry out his part in Pappy's plot. He was, of course, as ignorant as the three pilots of the scheme. Everything went smoothly until the party hit its high point about midnight. One of the gang had been a highly-rated fullback on one of the Big Ten teams. He was demonstrating a line buck that a few years before had netted five yards and a touchdown that meant a championship. The other two were cast in the role of the opposing line. The ex-fullback plunged through according to plan but kept on going and crashed up against the plasterboard wall shattering one of the sections and leaving an ugly gaping hole and strewing broken plaster over the major's floor.

The party stopped. A council of war was held to decide what should be done. It would never do to embarrass Pappy after he had gotten his friend to let them have the room. The plasterboard panels, about three feet square, were outlined by wood strips which held them in place and at the same time served as a crude sort of decoration. By removing these strips, the section of plasterboard could be fairly easily taken out. The walls in Pappy's room were of the same construction. To the trio, that appeared to be the logical place to get the material to make the necessary repairs to the major's wall.

Luckily Pappy had a tool kit in his room, and by morning the broken panel had been replaced, the wood strips nailed back in place and the room swept and tidied up so that no one would ever suspect that it had been occupied during the major's absence. They debated whether or not to leave a note to Pappy apologizing for the missing panel in his room but finally decided to forget it. As a matter of fact, it was quite easy at that stage of the party for them to forget almost everything. The broken pieces of plasterboard, sweepings, empty bottles, and other debris were carefully wrapped in a bundle to be deposited in some vacant lot on the way to the airdrome. They packed up, caught the early morning bus to Archer Field, and took off for New Guinea.

By this time Pappy's worries were beginning to get the best of him. He was imagining all kinds of possible complications that might have resulted. He hadn't confided his plot to anyone, and the whole 3rd Group wondered what had happened to the usually talkative, voluble Pappy, who moped around the camp all day. For the past three days there had been no stories and no jokes.

Sunday afternoon he could stand it no longer. He would fly back to Australia and find out what had happened. He and Sergeant Evans had just started getting his plane ready for the take-off when the cargo plane from Brisbane landed. The three participants in the comedy got out, walked over to Pappy, and thanked him profusely for fixing them up with the two hotel rooms during their leave. They had enjoyed themselves thoroughly, but they wouldn't have had half as good a time if it hadn't been for his thoughtfulness. They sure did appreciate it and hoped they could do something for him sometime.

The puzzled Pappy graciously accepted their thanks and said he was glad to have had the chance to help them. As soon as he could get away from them, he and the sergeant got aboard his B- 2 5 and headed for Brisbane. He had to get back and solve the mystery. Something had evidently gone wrong but the only way to find out what had happened was to go back to that hotel.

That evening, when Pappy came into the hotel lobby, the quartermaster major greeted him. His manner was so friendly that Pappy was suspicious until he casually mentioned that he had just returned that afternoon from Sydney as he had been delayed longer than he had expected. The two chatted affably for a while, and then Pappy headed upstairs to his room still a bit mystified but relieved to find out that his plot had not gotten anyone in trouble. He didn't care anything about the major, but after all those kids from the 3rd Group were his pals.

Unfortunately there was no one present to hear his remarks when he opened the door to his room and found the three-foot-square hole in his wall staring at him. He was probably somewhat annoyed, but the next day he managed to locate a sheet of plasterboard and made the repair himself. His annoyance couldn't have been very deep, however, as a few days later he told me the whole story as a joke on himself. He still didn't know why the panel was missing from his room, but on his next trip to New Guinea he asked his "guests" about it. When they told him, he laughed and said, "Well, I guess the joke is on me." He then outlined the rest of the story, even confessing that he had worried for three days about them. The gang enjoyed the recital as much as any of Pappy's fantastic yarns, but it was the last time they tried to play a practical joke on him. As for Pappy, as far as I know, it was the first, last, and only attempt on his part to get even with anyone.

14. "I TAUGHT HIM HOW TO FLY"

IN THE FALL of 1943 we got some information to the effect that the Japs had a couple of aircraft carriers moving south from their big base at Truk in the Caroline Island group, and probably headed for their big base at Rabaul on the island of New Britain. Our reconnaissance aircraft scoured the area for days but found no trace of the Jap vessels. It turned out to be just one of those rumours that seem to spring up without reason in time of war. Pappy had been doing more than his share of flying day and night looking for the target everyone wanted to get a crack at.

One day a lot of the crews of the 3rd Attack Group were sitting around in the operations tent at Dobodura on the north coast of New Guinea waiting for a break in the weather. It was raining as it can rain only in the tropics and the clouds were almost down on the ground. As Pappy said, "Today even the birds are walking."

The conversation drifted around to the subject of aircraft carriers. Quite a few of them, both ours and the Japs, had been sunk so far in the war and aircraft had been responsible. The kids heard that Pappy had once been a navy flier and they were trying to egg him into a story on the subject. He listened to the discussion for quite a while without saying anything. Just as the gang was about to decide that Pappy was not in the mood to entertain them, he cleared his throat and leaned forward in his chair. All conversation ceased. They had gotten their wish.

"Yes," said Pappy, "this carrier operation has a lot of problems connected with it. It reminds me of the time during the Battle of the Coral Sea last year. I was on the Saratoga at the time as a sort of adviser on account of all the experience I have had with carriers. There I was standing on the bridge with Admiral Bill Halsey. I taught him how to fly. I said, 'Bill, you'd better' ...'"

One of the newly arrived youngsters interrupted. An old-timer sitting alongside him nudged him to keep quiet, but the kid went on. "Why, Colonel Gunn," he said, "Admiral Halsey wasn't in the Battle of the Coral Sea and neither was the Saratoga."

Pappy glared at him, somewhat annoyed at the interruption, but quickly recovered and started to cover up his error.

"Come to think of it you're right, son," he said. "You see I know all these admirals and sometimes I get them mixed up. It wasn't Admiral Halsey at that. It was Admiral Frank Fletcher. I taught him how to fly and the carrier was the Lexington. Well, there I was standing on the bridge of the Lexington with Fletcher and I said, 'Fletch, don't you think you should' ..."

The interruption was repeated. Once again the old-timers tried to stop it, but the youngster persisted. "But, Colonel Gunn, wasn't the Lexington sunk at the Coral Sea Battle? Were you on board at that time?"

For a second Pappy was taken aback. Was someone questioning his veracity? Why, it was unthinkable. Still, he wasn't going to be stopped by some trifling inaccuracy.

"No, son," he continued, "I wasn't ever sunk with my ship. I just named the wrong battle, that's all. You see, I've been in all these battles and on all these carriers, and for a minute I forgot that the episode I want to tell you about actually happened during the Battle of Midway. Yes, it was the Battle of Midway, that's what it was, and it was the Yorktown, yes, that's what it was, and Admiral Marc Mitscher was commanding. Well, I was on the Yorktown at the time standing there on the bridge with Mitscher. I taught him how to fly, too. We were moving out to meet the Jap fleet going at top speed and I said to the admiral, 'Mitsch,' I said, 'we ought to be launching our planes' ..."

The interruption came this time from one of the old-timers who had decided that Pappy was getting in too deep and needed rescuing. Besides, if he could divert Pappy into another story nothing would be lost. They were all good.

"Pappy," he said, "don't you remember the date of the Battle of Midway?"

Pappy was incensed at the attack from this quarter. And from one of the old gang, his friends, it was intolerable.

"What the hell has the date got to do with it?" he roared. "Do you think I'm an almanac or something? Why should I bother to keep all the dates in my head of all the battles I've been in?"

"But, Pappy," his heckler persisted, "the Battle of Midway was fought on June 5, last year. Don't you remember we were on leave in Sydney that day sitting in the cocktail room at the Australia House when that big Aussie clobbered you because he thought you were winking at his girl?"

"What do you mean he clobbered me?" yelled Pappy. "He didn't lay a finger on me. You were there and you saw me beat hell out of him and chase him and his girl both out of the hotel. She gave me more trouble than he did, scratching and kicking like a —"

Suddenly he realized that he had ruined his own original story. The scowl and jutting lower lip told the gang they had gone too far. Now he really was mad. This unheard-of interference was no longer to be tolerated.

"All right," he growled, "if I can't talk around here without being interrupted by a bunch of brats, to hell with you! It looks like you're too smart to listen for fear you might learn something."

He stalked out of the tent. It was a couple of days before he would even speak to any of the group. Old-timers and the newly arrived members alike learned their lesson. Never again was Pappy interrupted, let alone having the accuracy of one of his stories questioned.

15. THE WICKED DIGIT

A FEW DAYS later Pappy transferred his annoyance with the 3rd Attack Group to something that had bothered him for more than a month. Somehow he had broken the little finger on his right hand between the second and third joints. One of the doctors in Brisbane had set it in a splint at least three times as Pappy would forget about it and bang it into something and break the splint loose or impatiently tear it off. He made a metal protector for the cast but that didn't help much. Then he tried taping the offending little finger and third finger together. This expedient didn't last long, as it was not only clumsy but it got in the way and prevented him from using his hand. That was something that Pappy couldn't stand for, and he decided to remedy the situation at once.

He hunted up his friend Major John "Doc" Gilmore, the flight surgeon of the 3rd Group then at Dobodura and said, "Doc, I want you to cut this damn finger off. I don't need a little finger anyhow, and this thing won't heal up. It keeps bothering me all the time. I got work to do, so cut it off."

Gilmore tried to calm Pappy down. He explained that if the finger was immobilized for a couple of weeks, it would get all right but the trouble was it was being kept irritated the way Pappy was acting. He further stated that any hand, including Pappy's, ought to have five fingers, and that he was not going to cut it off.

"What do you mean a couple of weeks?" returned Pappy. "The trouble with you pill-pushing veterinaries is that you're not only ignorant and don't seem to know that I got a war to fight, but you're chicken. Afraid of a little blood, that's what you are. So you won't cut it off. Well, I'll fix it for you."

He calmly drew his pistol from the shoulder holster, shifted it to his left hand, and pointed it at the offending digit.

"If you won't cut it off," he said, "I'll shoot it off, and then maybe your humanitarian instincts will induce you to finish the job."

Gilmore had known Pappy now for more than a year. He also knew that Pappy would carry out his threat and it would be a far messier job than a simple amputation. Further remonstration was useless. "Well?" said Pappy as Gilmore hesitated.

"All right," the doctor replied, "come on over to the hospital and we'll get it over with."

On arrival at the hospital Pappy was given a local anaesthetic and the offending finger removed. The doctor gave him a sedative, told him to go to bed, and let him see the job the next morning.

Around noon the next day at mess Gilmore inquired for Pappy, as he had not shown up.

"Oh," was the reply from the Group Operations officer, "Colonel Gunn left for Australia this morning at five-thirty."

"Who did he go with?" asked the doctor.

"Oh, he and that sergeant of his took off in his B-25," was the reply.

"Well," said the doctor, "you don't have to be crazy to be a good aviator, but I guess it helps."

A few days later Pappy was back at Dobodura. He was accustomed to having a fair-sized welcoming group whenever the word came in that he was about to land. There was always the chance that he might have a new story or maybe a different version of one of the old ones. Those were good, too.

This time, however, the crowd was much larger than usual. Every officer of the group who was not flying a mission seemed to be there. They gathered around Pappy, formed a parade, and led him to the big thatched hut that they called "Club Tropicana" on the edge of the jungle about a quarter of a mile from the flying field. In a cleared-off area in front of the entrance was a small casket by the side of an open grave. With all the proper pomp and ceremony, the "burial" rites were now performed on what purported to be the amputated little finger of Pappy Gunn. The "headstone," fashioned from a block of native mahogany, was then erected over the grave bearing the carved inscription, "The Wicked Digit of Pappy, Departed This Life October 20, 1943. Requiescat in Pace."

The "honoured guest" enjoyed the whole thing immensely. He seemed to take it as some form of personal tribute and recognition. It wasn't long before he added the story to his repertoire, with graphic descriptions of all the events leading up to the operation, the operation itself, and the final interment by the 3rd Attack Group in the little grave in the New Guinea jungle.

After the war was over Pappy always insisted that the mahogany marker was still there and that the natives had made a shrine out of it. This is one of Pappy's stories that I want to believe. Somehow I like to feel that there still remains a memento of one of the most colourful and likable heroes of the Pacific war in that little open patch of cleared jungle near Dobodura, the scene of so many of his exploits.

16. BACK TO THE PHILIPPINES

BY THE MIDDLE of September 1944 the decision had been made to return to the Philippines on October 20. The landing was to be on the island of Leyte, in the vicinity of the port of Tacloban, in Leyte Gulf, on the east coast. In the meantime we started working on the oil refineries and storage tanks at Balikpapan on the island of Borneo, from which the Japs got most of their aviation gasoline. We knew they had more than three thousand airplanes in the Philippines and we wanted to stop their fuel supply and keep as many of them on the ground as possible when we went ashore.

As soon as Pappy heard the news, his fertile brain began producing. His first scheme was to let him take one of the B-25's that we had remodelled to carry twelve forward-firing 50-caliber machine guns, fly it to Manila, and shoot up the three hundred Jap planes that our intelligence crowd said were parked wing tip to wing tip on both sides of Taft Boulevard. This street, which ran along Manila Bay, was straight for about two miles and the Japs were using it for a landing field and for storage of airplanes. An attack would certainly pay off, but the trouble was, we didn't have any airplane with range enough to make the round trip, even from our most forward airdrome at Biak, in Dutch New Guinea. This didn't bother Pappy, however. His plan was to arrive over Manila just at daybreak and, using incendiary ammunition and bombs, burn up every airplane on Taft Boulevard. He admitted that he couldn't make it all the way home, but had the place marked on the map for me where he would run out of fuel, ditch the B-25, and be picked up by one of our rescue amphibians, or maybe I could arrange with the Navy to have a submarine make a rendezvous with him. The spot he pointed out to me was more than five hundred miles short of home. I vetoed the idea.

A couple of days later Pappy was back in my headquarters again.

"General," he said, "you can't turn me down this time. I've got it all figured out. I'll fly the B-25 alone. That will save some weight. The top gun turret won't be necessary, so I'll take that out and save another couple of thousand pounds. Then, the incendiaries from the machine guns will do the job, so I won't need to carry another ton of bombs. With all that weight saved I'll rig up a couple of three hundred-gallon gas tanks and hang them one on each wing and it figures I can make the round trip. How about it, General?"

Pappy almost wept when I turned this scheme down, too. I explained to him that I couldn't afford to take even one of our B-25's out of action for two or three weeks while he made all the changes in it for his bright idea. In the meantime, Admiral Halsey's carriers were scheduled to make a couple of raids on the Jap airdromes around Manila and, furthermore, his figures on the projected range of his remodelled B-25 didn't allow for any margin of safety. If he ran into head winds either coming or going he would wind up landing in the Pacific Ocean. Then we would lose the airplane, and if the water was too rough for one of our flying boats to land we would lose him, too. Pappy left completely dejected but was back the next day.

This time he had decided to become a ground soldier. The idea was that I would make a deal with the Navy to put him on a submarine which would set him ashore in a rubber boat some night on the east coast of Leyte about twenty miles south of Tacloban. I was also to get a letter from General MacArthur instructing him to organize an army of Filipinos to attack the Japs from the rear as we made our landing on the shore of Leyte Gulf. With his knowledge of the country and the people, and armed with General MacArthur's letter as credentials, to Pappy there was no doubt as to the virtue of his scheme or the prospect of a brilliant and successful operation.

For the next half-hour I tried to explain to Pappy that we had more than half a million troops out there who might resent his winning the war single-handed. Furthermore, it was rather doubtful whether the Navy could recall a submarine at this late date just to carry him to Leyte and, even if they did, he wouldn't have time to recruit and train his private army before the twentieth of October when we were due to land there. He started to talk about the guerrillas who were all ready to go into action if he could just get there to lead them, but I solved the problem by giving him another job.

"Pappy," I said, "I want you to recruit from the maintenance outfit back in Australia a special picked gang of about fifty men who can do anything. They must be able to shoot, dig slit trenches, build a shack to live in, lay steel mat for a runway, rebuild wrecked airplanes, overhaul engines, live off the country, and fight with fists, knives, or rocks. When we go ashore we are going to be working on a shoestring and we are going to need some smart tough guys like you to keep going. I'm going to move that outfit out of Australia soon anyhow, but in the meantime go on down there and train fifty real shock troops for me. I'll want them up here by the thirteenth of October to load on a boat, so get going."

Pappy grinned happily and took off. On the afternoon of the twelfth, two C-47 transports landed at Hollandia near my headquarters. Pappy had sent a message that he was coming in with his gang, so I went down to the field to look them over. He had done the job. They looked tough enough to take care of themselves anywhere. Each one was armed with a pistol and a trench knife and carried a good-sized bag slung over his shoulder. I asked Pappy what was in the bags. "Tools and spare ammunition," replied Pappy. "General," he went on, "these boys are what you asked for. They can do anything you want done, and if any Japs start interfering with them, they can handle that job, too. What do you want me to do with them?"

I attached Pappy and his gang to the Air Task Force commanded by Colonel "Dave" Hutchison, which would go ashore to organize the airdrome as soon as the place was captured. That night they loaded for the Philippines.

On October 20 four American divisions stormed ashore near Tacloban and at Dulag a town about twenty miles to the south. Both places had an airdrome that the Japs had been using but they were badly pitted from the bombing by Halsey's carrier boys and both were too small for the number of airplanes I intended to put on them.

By the next day General Verne Mudge's 1st Cavalry Division had captured the Tacloban strip and the bulldozers and graders went to work filling up the bomb craters and getting the ground levelled off. The place was nothing but a sand spit a little more than a mile long and about three hundred yards wide. We would have to cover it with steel mat, and before that was laid we needed some coral or rock ballast on top of the existing soil to keep the steel mat from buckling under the impact of airplanes landing on it.

Pappy told us of a coral deposit about two miles away and we started hauling it to the strip the next day when the trucks got unloaded. In the meantime his "spearhead" outfit had already patched up some wrecked Jap sheds on the edge of the field for use as repair shops later on and were constructing a control tower out of palm-tree logs to handle the traffic as soon as we were ready to fly in our airplanes. In anticipation of Jap bombing, they took care to dig plenty of slit trenches near where they were working. A couple of days later I admired this latter job tremendously when the Japs pulled a bombing raid while I was inspecting the construction work at the field.

Pappy was an invaluable man to have on this job. As soon as the steel mat was ashore and enough of the surface ready he showed up with about two hundred Filipinos and members of some Chinese Youth Society and put them to work carrying the heavy sheets of steel mat over where our men could fasten them in place. Each day he recruited more local labour until finally we had more than fifteen hundred Filipinos on the job. Pappy was all over the place, keeping things moving and working himself harder than anyone else.

The Japs didn't ignore us by any means. For the first five days they bombed us four or five times during daylight and generally twice at night. We had managed to set up a radar which gave us about fifteen minutes' warning but to Pappy that didn't mean stopping work. Everyone stayed on the job until the Jap airplanes appeared and then dived for the nearest slit trench. As soon as the bombs hit, Pappy would jump up and yell "Come on, let's get back to work and get this field fixed up so our planes can come up here and chase those bow-legged so and sos away." The quotation is not exactly what Pappy actually said, but it expresses what he meant.

We had about five hundred feet of steel mat in place when I got a hurry-up call from Colonel Hutchison. Twenty-four landing craft had beached on the edge of the strip and unloaded supplies, guns, ammunition, and troops right on the airdrome, stopping all work. Another twenty-eight ships were reported coming in during the night to do the same thing. I went out to the strip to look over the situation. The place was a mess, all cluttered up with troops, trucks, crates, and boxes piled six to ten feet high. The only item I could not find was more steel mat which we needed to complete surfacing the airdrome.

I got hold of one of the army brigadier generals who was looking after the unloading of supplies and told him to hurry up and clear the airdrome. We would help with all the military and civilian man power we had, but beginning the next morning Colonel Hutchison would take his bulldozers and push back into the water anything still left on the place which interfered with getting an airdrome built. In the meantime, we were setting up machine guns on the beach with Pappy Gunn in charge, with orders to stop any more landing craft from coming ashore. Pappy had volunteered for the job, giving as his reason that being an old navy man he was the best one qualified to meet such a situation.

To make sure that my action was legalized and that no more stuff would be moved in on the Tacloban strip, I saw General MacArthur and told him what I had done. He immediately passed the word to both the army and navy commanders that he wanted the place used as an airdrome, not as an unloading point. Actually all these supplies belonged at a point on the beach about five miles south of the airdrome but the ship captains wanted to unload anywhere they could and get away from the beach before some Jap aviator bombed them while they were sitting ducks and unable to dodge. I couldn't blame them for feeling that way, but we needed an airdrome, and we needed it quickly.

We mobilized every soldier and Filipino we could get our hands on and started clearing the strip. By morning we were beginning once again to make an airdrome and two more barge loads of steel mat had arrived to start the final surfacing.

General MacArthur's orders had stopped any more unloading of supplies except for these two barges so that Pappy's machine guns were not needed to preserve the peace. He acted as though he was disappointed at losing this opportunity to use them, but actually he and the rest of us were so anxious to get the airdrome in operation that he forgot all about the incident and went back to work harder than ever.

A few days later Admiral Halsey commanding the 3rd Fleet supporting the Leyte landing lost the aircraft carrier Princeton. He radioed us that he was sending about thirty of the carrier's aircraft to Tacloban, as he had no room for them with his fleet. It would be just after dark when they came in to land and we had only about fifteen hundred feet of the airdrome completed and no landing lights. We notified him of the situation but it was too late. The planes were on their way. The next thing we knew they were radioing for landing instructions. By this time it was dark with low clouds, a thousand feet of ceiling, and drizzling rain.

Pappy came up with the bright idea of tying flashlights to a couple of sticks with which to signal the planes to a landing. He said that as he was a graduate of the Pensacola Naval Training Station and had a lot of carrier training, he could bring them in. We told him to go ahead. Pappy's improvised system worked and all of Halsey's planes got down safely.

The navy planes came in in flights of six. Three of the flights had already landed, when the fourth flight began to circle the airdrome with their landing gears down and their running lights on. I was standing there with Colonel Hutchison watching Pappy with his improvised signalling equipment and admiring the job he was doing. As the first plane landed we suddenly realized that there were still six planes up there in the circle. A Jap light bomber had tagged on to the end of the formation in the dark and had let down his landing gear and turned on his lights like the rest. Just then, instead of landing, the Jap who was the next plane in position to turn in for his final approach headed out over the water, slapped his bombs into a big landing craft loaded with drums of gasoline, and got away. Pappy's landing job for the rest of the aircraft was made much easier. We didn't need any landing lights for the next half-hour.

We got our airplanes on the Tacloban strip on October 27. Thirty-four P-38 fighters from my crack 49th Group flew in and our troubles were over. The Japs made an occasional raid after that, but their unopposed field days were over. We also flew in plenty of mechanics and supply men, and Pappy's men became guards around the airdrome. We had already picked up a couple of Japs just outside the airdrome who were wearing Filipino clothes, and with all the local labour working there, we didn't dare to take chances on sabotage. The boys took the guard duty in their stride like everything else. Pappy had done a real job for us when he selected and trained that outfit.

As soon as we got the Tacloban strip in shape for operations Pappy began to get impatient to get into the war again. He started by trying to argue Colonel Hutchison into letting him have a B-25 bomber to pull a solo raid on Manila. From talking with the Filipinos around Tacloban he was sure he knew where the headquarters of the Japanese commander, General Yamishita, was, and one bomb might eliminate him and wind up the war. Not having any luck with Hutchison, he appealed to me. I reminded Pappy that General MacArthur had declared Manila an open city so that we couldn't drop bombs there anyhow. Furthermore, killing a top commander wouldn't be enough even to slow down the war, let alone end it. We had shot down the number-one Jap Admiral Yamamoto back in 1943, but it didn't stop the Jap Navy from operating. Besides, the mission Pappy wanted to try was a suicide job anyhow and with his knowledge of the Philippine Islands and the people, he was worth more to me alive than any Jap general dead. The thing that finally quieted him down, however, was when I asked him what would happen to his family at Santo Tomas if he were shot down and his body identified, or if he were captured and tortured into talking. This really began to worry him. He became so afraid that the Japs would find out that he was alive and with us at Tacloban, and would either kill his family or move them out of the Philippines, that from then on he avoided all the press correspondents as if they had the plague.

Colonel Hutchison played it safe and to make sure that Pappy stayed out of trouble, he issued a direct order to him not to fly without his permission and passed the word to everyone else on the field to watch Pappy to see that he didn't steal an airplane. "Hutch" told me that he was sure if he ever allowed Pappy to go out with a bombing formation, the next thing he'd hear would be that Pappy had become "lost" from the mission he was supposed to be on and had ended by dropping his load on the Japanese Army headquarters in Manila.

On the afternoon of October 30 I was out on the airdrome with Colonel Woods, our boss engineer, with a map of the area spread out on the top of my jeep explaining where I wanted an extension of airplane parking space constructed when I happened to look up. About five hundred yards away, just lifting over the palm trees at the south end of the strip, were four Jap planes abreast with the lights beginning to twinkle from the machine guns mounted in the wings. They had come in low and the radar had not picked them up, so we had no warning of the attack. Woods and I dropped flat on the ground behind the jeep as the Japs swept along the runway strafing and dropping bombs. The jeep didn't get touched but a truck ten feet away had its tires punctured, the gas tanks set on fire, and the driver wounded. Two men were killed in an anti-aircraft machine-gun pit about fifty feet to one side of us. Two airplanes were set on fire and destroyed and two other men working on the strip were killed and ten more wounded.

One of the wounded was Lieutenant Colonel Paul I. "Pappy" Gunn. He and Colonel Hutchison had also dived under a jeep but it didn't give much protection. A piece of phosphorus from one of the Japs' incendiary bombs struck Pappy and imbedded itself in the upper part of his left arm. We rushed him over to the field hospital, but before the surgeon could dig the fragment out of his arm the damage had been done. The phosphorus had burned deep into the flesh, severing nerves, muscles, and arteries in the process. That night even Pappy could not stand the pain and had to be given sedatives. The next morning we had him flown to Brisbane, Australia, where our best hospital, the 42nd General, was located, to see what they could do for him. We couldn't get word to his wife Polly, so we wired his sister Jewell, whom Pappy had designated as the next of kin to be notified in case he became a member of the dead, wounded, or missing list.

Pappy was out of the war. I hated to lose him, but the kids missed him, too. Pappy's stories would be told and retold for years, but they wouldn't be told as the old master could tell them.

I think the one who probably missed him most was Sergeant Evans who had been with him since he and Pappy had practically adopted each other back in Australia when they had both been in the 3rd Attack Group at Charters Towers.

Evans had worked with Pappy, flown with him on test flights and combat flights as co-pilot, machine gunner, flight engineer, or any other job that was assigned him by his boss. He would tell you that Pappy was not only the best pilot in the Air Force but the only one he would fly with. Pappy worked him like a slave, cursed him constantly, and swore by him. When Evans said the airplane was ready to fly, Pappy climbed aboard and was ready to take it off without question. The two were inseparable and when Pappy was knocked out of the war I knew I had to do something about Sergeant Evans.

He wanted to be a pilot, so I sent him back to the States to take the officer-training course and get flying training. He made the grade, got his wings and a commission as second lieutenant in the Air Force. By that time the war had ended, but Evans decided to remain in the service.

Some time in 1947 I learned that he had been killed in an airplane accident. He had wanted to go home from the Philippines and get flying training but somehow I wished that instead I had sent him home for discharge as unfit for further military service owing to tropical fatigue or kept him with me as a chauffeur or something until the war ended. I know he wouldn't have liked it but perhaps he would be alive today if I had simply told him to forget about Pappy and go back to work.

17. LIBERATION AND REUNION

ON JANUARY 9, 1945, four divisions of MacArthur's Sixth Army landed at Lingayan Gulf on the main island of Luzon and started the final drive to recapture Manila, about one hundred and fifty miles to the south, and liberate the Philippines. The troops moved steadily ahead against stiff opposition until January 31, when we got word that the Japs had quit feeding about three thousand seven hundred internees held at Santo Tomas University in Manila as well as several hundred military prisoners in the old Bilibid Prison. In their already-weakened condition, after three years on little more than starvation rations, it was doubtful whether they could survive much longer.

General Mac Arthur sent for Major General Verne Mudge, commanding the crack motorized 1st Cavalry Division, and told him to drive for Manila at top speed and rescue the internees and prisoners at Santo Tomas and Bilibid. Mudge moved out at midnight, February 1, headed for his objective eighty miles away.

Fighting off small bodies of Jap troops that tried to delay him, Mudge smashed his way forward and at 8: 30 p.m. on the third his armoured cars clattered into the courtyard of Santo Tomas. The internees were ready and expectant. Just at dusk one of our planes had flown over the university grounds and dropped a message attached to a pair of pilot's goggles. It read, "Roll out the barrel. Santa Claus is coming to town Sunday or Monday." This was Sunday.

With the 1st Cavalry Division that evening was Colonel Dave Hutchison who had promised Pappy just before Gunn was evacuated to Australia that he would personally go to Santo Tomas and take care of Polly and the children, who had been interned there since January 1942, when the Japs captured Manila. "Hutch" kept his promise. He found them immediately after the American troops entered the university grounds, told them that Pappy had been injured, and that he was now in Australia. He also said that arrangements had already been made to fly them all to Brisbane, where Pappy was hospitalized. It was the first news Polly had that Pappy had been wounded or that he had even been engaging in combat with the American Air Force. Another one of those rescued was Pappy's old maintenance officer at the beginning of the war, Lieutenant Dan Stickle.

Dan was in pretty bad shape when we found him. Between malnutrition and dysentery he had lost a lot of weight and had to be hospitalized for more than four months. Just about the time he was ready for active duty again, the war ended and Dan got a discharge to go back to work on his old job with Philippine Air Lines.

Polly Gunn and the four children all showed the effects of more than three years of living close to the starvation line. Polly's normal weight of around one hundred and twelve pounds had dropped to eighty-three pounds. Constance, now twenty-one, Julie, nineteen, Paul, Junior, seventeen, and Nathaniel, fifteen, all looked as though they needed a couple of months of square meals. Right after Pappy left Manila on Christmas Day, 1941, the Japs had stepped up their bombing attacks around Nichols Field, and as some of the bombs were landing near where the Gunns lived in Paranaque, Polly and the youngsters had moved to a house in the little town of Calonwan just south of Manila. A few days later, when General MacArthur declared Manila an open city and started evacuating his troops to Bataan and Corregidor, everyone figured that the city was now safe so Polly and the family took a house in Manila, a few blocks from city hall.

On New Year's Day the Japs entered the city. Polly and the family went to church that morning and then came back home, like everyone else, to wait. No one knew how the Japs would behave or what they would do with the foreigners living in Manila. The only sensible thing to do seemed to be to stay indoors and see what would happen.

Three days later a Japanese captain, a lieutenant, and four soldiers knocked on the door and then searched the house from one end to the other. They interrogated Polly and the children for about an hour, asking them among other things where her husband was. Polly told them that Pappy had joined the Army but had been killed in an airplane accident about three weeks before and that there had been no other news as the airplane had crashed in the water and no bodies had been recovered. She had impressed upon the youngsters that they must stick to the same story. They all did.

Polly couldn't give them any military information, as she didn't know any. After making sure that there were no American soldiers hiding in the house and satisfied that Polly and the children were telling the truth, the captain told her that the family would be interned in Santo Tomas

University with the rest of the foreigners. He said to stay in the house in the meantime until further orders.

No one bothered them again until the sixteenth of January 1942, when the Japanese consul, Ito, came to see them. He angrily told Polly that she was supposed to be in Santo Tomas by the fifteenth and wanted to know why she hadn't obeyed orders. Polly explained that she had been ordered by the Jap captain, whose name she didn't know, to stay indoors and that no one had come to give her any further instructions. Ito told her to get packed, ready to move, and that some soldiers would be along later to take her to the internment camp. The family could take just one suitcase for the five of them.

They packed the suitcase with food and a few articles of clothing and waited. A Russian boy working at a local grocery store brought them some more food and told them that they would be wise to take all they could with them as the Japs were furnishing no rations to the internees. The suitcase was hurriedly repacked. This time it held nothing but food. On January 20, a Jap truck with two soldiers put an end to the suspense of the past four days when they drove up to the house, loaded the family and its suitcase aboard, and took them off to Santo Tomas to join more than three thousand other internees who were to call the university home for the next three years.

Through the Philippine Red Cross and friends and an occasional ration doled out by the Japanese they managed to keep alive but not much more. In October that first year Julie developed an ulcer on her spine. Malnutrition did not help any and the condition got steadily worse until she had lost the use of her legs and had to stay in bed. Polly finally argued the Jap commandant into letting her go to St. Luke's Hospital where a Philippine doctor treated her and put her in a cast from her hips to her chest. With a little better food ration at the hospital she gradually got back the use of her legs but wore the cast for nearly a year longer. As soon as she could get around under her own power, the Japs allowed her to visit Santo Tomas to renew her pass and see her family. Julie took advantage of these trips to smuggle in money and little items such as tooth paste which she obtained from Filipino friends and which she could hide in the cast.

In early 1944 Julie had substituted a brace for the cast and the Japs sent her back to Santo Tomas where she joined the rest of the family. She was still wearing the brace when our troops liberated Manila on February 3, 1945.

Following Pappy's instructions, Polly never tried to find out where he was or whether he was even alive, but in the early days in Santo Tomas every once in a while some internee who had been brought to Manila from the southern islands told her of Pappy's daring exploits. Often they had seen him and received aid from him. One man wept when he told Polly what he knew and how much her son Paul looked like his father. Most of the messages were slow getting to her and almost anything could have happened in the interim, but she remained confident that Pappy would overcome every obstacle and come back to her. Besides, she and the children did a lot of praying.

Bits of information came in later during the last year of their imprisonment. There weren't many of them, and they came from totally unexpected sources, but they served to buoy up the hopes of the Gunn family and make it easier to bear the hardships of the prison camp and the brutality of their captors.

One day a Filipino girl whom Polly did not even know had obtained a pass on some pretext or other to enter Santo Tomas and had sent a message that Pappy was safe. When Polly tried to talk to her, however, the girl avoided her. She probably was afraid to be seen talking to an American woman, as the Japs might have become suspicious that a message was being communicated. If that happened, both the messenger and Polly would probably have been subjected to questioning under torture to get the contents of the message and the name of the sender.

Again, a young Filipino told her that a man in the camp hospital had a message for her. The man was in a secluded corner in the hospital surrounded by a screen. She was cautioned to watch for an opportunity to walk past his bed, slip briefly in behind the screen, and leave immediately. She was not to talk to him or even appear to be interested in him. The Japs had planted some pro-Nipponese Filipinos all over the place as orderlies, workmen, and cleaning women, and she mustn't take any chances.

Polly followed directions. The man who had the message was a Filipino who had been suspected of communicating with the guerrillas who operated in the jungles and mountains east of Manila. He had been horribly beaten and was lying on his stomach on the cot unable to move, but still conscious. His back was a crisscross of bloody welts where the bamboo rods had been at work trying to get a confession out of him. Polly walked through the hospital in the direction of the screened cot. Watching carefully as she passed by, she slipped in behind the screen and knelt down beside the beaten prisoner for a second or two. He whispered, "Your husband is alive and well." Polly straightened up and walked away without a glance in his direction and went back to her family. She didn't even know the man.

The next news she had of Pappy was when she was rescued and we told her that he had been wounded three months before and was now in the army hospital in Brisbane, Australia.

Polly had not had an easy time of it during those three years but she met every situation like a veteran. The big problem had been one of survival for her four children as well as for herself. In spite of almost continual sickness and the difficulties of getting sufficient food to stay alive, she had never lost hope. She had met the problem and solved it somehow. None of the family was in good shape when rescued, but they were alive. That was the main thing. Let Polly tell a little of her story of three years in a prison camp, where every day was different and exciting and frightening, but most of the time filled with worry.

"We came to appreciate the importance of each day. Even death ceased to take on such an awesome aspect.

"We stood in line perpetually — lines for the shower, lines for the bathroom, for medical care, food, to wash one's hair, launder one's clothes — always lines. There were rumours, roll calls, unexpected inspections, occasionally at two or three o'clock in the morning — we never knew why or when. All annoying, but in a way trivial.

"There was sufficient food in the beginning, then less and less, and finally months of starvation. Many persons supplemented the meagre ration issued by the Japs by eating weeds, leaves, and bulbs. I was always impressed, however, by the courage of the majority of the internees, particularly the women, who kept their humour, continued to keep themselves looking as nice as possible, cared for their children, and calmly accepted their assignments of work along with the men.

"The Gunns had to go all out in the illness department. Not just the usual dysentery, dengue fever, beriberi, flu, and itches. They plagued all of us all the time. Besides these there were plaster casts, operations, and diseases that resulted and required more operations several years afterward.

"Constance and Nathaniel each had appendectomies performed during the period of starvation. Paul injured his back carrying large kettles of hot rice while working in the kitchen. Julie was in a plaster cast for eighteen months and then wore a brace up to the time we were liberated. During that time, on her occasional trips from the hospital to our prison camp, she became the best little spy to be found anywhere — at the tender age of sixteen. The cast afforded her an opportunity to conceal money and messages, not only helping her own family, but other prisoners as well. She even braved walking the streets wearing the arm band of identification which many of the Filipinos regarded as a badge of valour.

"We were helped secretly with money, food, and medicine by a number of Spanish friends, Swiss friends, a Russian family, an Austrian family, and three padres of Santo Tomas Seminary.

"My children were all courageous. We faced many problems together. It was most difficult to tell them, when they were starving, that we would be better for the refining this experience would bring, but they listened. I was determined we would leave Santo Tomas having no bitter outlook. To me those things were part of, and the result of, war. Many times in the night, when I'd hear a Japanese plane coming in, in stormy weather, trying to find a hole in the clouds to come through to land, I would find myself sympathetic.

"The liberation was not so sweet as we had expected. Manila was in flames, our friends in distress, and we were so disappointed not to see P. I. when the soldiers came in. When we learned that he was wounded, we were frantic to find out the extent of his injuries. Everyone was very nice but we did not breathe easy again until we reached Brisbane, where he was hospitalized, and got the family united again. It had been a long time."

There isn't much doubt that it was Polly's courage, devotion, and real nerve that brought the family through an experience that would have licked anyone of lesser fibre. The job she did made a tremendous impression on all four of the children. Julie sums up the prevailing attitude:

"To me the most amazing thing about our stay in Santo Tomas was my mother's nerve. With the worry of my dad she also had to take care of the four of us children under the conditions in a prison camp. She had always been quite capable but leaned heavily on my dad. But when I became ill in the camp, she really went to war. She talked to doctors, men on the American Committee, and Japanese until I was given a pass to go to a hospital out of the camp. One man on the American Committee began calling her 'Two-Gun.' After I was put into a plaster body cast and could make trips into the camp to get my pass extended or my address changed, she would sit in the Japanese office with me as cool as a cucumber while she passed notes for me to take out in my cast and receive the incoming money and notes. After a year in the cast I was put into a metal brace and returned to the camp for the duration. I was allowed to go with the last busload of sick people to the University of the Philippine General Hospital to have my brace adjusted. When my friends discovered I was there, they came with packages of food and notes and money for their friends or families in the camp. My family and I had planned for my brothers to take all my packages right after I passed the inside wall of the camp so I could then enter the Japanese office with only the notes and money on me. But this time the Japanese guards at the gate didn't let me enter the camp alone; they sent a guard with me. Mom walked right up to me, took my hand, and walked with me behind the little man with the big gun. The Japanese in the office went through everything I had and as they checked each item of food Mom made a sound of pure hunger. He gave back almost all the food and never searched my person. I often thought maybe it was her height that made her feel equal to our captors; she was on an eye level with most Japanese. She was never pessimistic. She always believed we would be reunited with my dad, saying that he would really take care of her when the war was over because she'd see to it that he did. Of course, when we all met, Dad was wounded and she babied him like she had never babied any of us children."

Connie still remembers Santo Tomas. Like the rest, the food problem impressed itself on her for life. "The food was never sufficient or palatable — the women joked while they picked the bugs and worms from the cracked wheat." There were other things too like clothes — she was a girl after all. "Clothes, after a three-year period and constant use, became a problem, not only because they were threadbare, but everyone had lost so much weight that nothing fitted."

With a touch of sadness she remembers the lack of understanding people had for the stories that perhaps the released prisoners wanted to tell so badly. After all they had had no one but themselves to talk to for over three years.

"No amount of explaining could properly describe our lives in Santo Tomas — people cut off from the world, slowly starving, without giving up hope of rescue, yet realizing their insignificance. Only those who had experienced it seemed to understand. Upon returning home, in spite of sincere inquiries, no one was capable of understanding, and because of this, they were not really interested."

She too pays a tribute to Polly:

"My mother, so weakened by beriberi that she could scarcely walk, was obliged to give up her dream of rest and quiet and take on still more responsibilities when we joined Dad in Brisbane."

She was quite a soldier in her own way — Mrs. Paul I. Gunn.

On the nineteenth of February we flew Polly and the children to Brisbane and the Gunn family was united again. Without thinking, I found that I had broken some rule of the Army Medical Department. Released prisoners and internees were supposed to be given a thorough physical examination and be kept under observation for a while before being released, but breaking a regulation seemed to fit any situation connected with Pappy, so I merely admitted my error and forgot about it.

Pappy had been having a miserable time in the hospital. The damage to the nerves in his arm had a peculiar effect. Certain high notes of someone whistling or singing or even a high soprano speaking voice would jangle something and nearly drive him crazy. His first nurse had a high soprano voice. Pappy sent for the doctor and demanded a nurse with a bass voice. The astounded medico tried to argue with Pappy but got nowhere, so he reported it to his senior medical officer. Another consultation with Pappy led to another report still higher up on the chain of command. Whether or not the doctors decided that there was a reason for his request the records do not show, but in order to keep peace in the hospital, Pappy finally got a nurse with a fairly deep voice and was given a room by himself where he could shut the door and keep out most of the nerve-irritating noises. In addition to the nerve damage, the circulation in his arm had been interfered with when the arteries and muscles were severed.

His fingers became numb and then the joints swelled and pained. The forearm, wrist, and fingers gradually lost colour and took on a waxen look that didn't add to Pappy's happiness or lessen his caustic remarks about the Army Medical Department. If you consider the extra aggravation caused by Pappy's normal temperament and his impatience with the doctors who couldn't fix him up so that he could get back in action it is no wonder that the staff at the 42nd General Hospital wished there was some other place to send him.

When Pappy and Polly were first married, twenty-two years before, she had weighed one hundred and twelve pounds, which Pappy decided was about right for a girl of her height of around five feet two inches. During their honeymoon, one day he had remarked, "Polly, you are just the right weight now, but I'm telling you that if you ever pass one hundred and twenty, I'm going to get a divorce."

Over the years the threat had become a Gunn family joke but at any event up to the time Pappy had last seen her that Christmas Day of 1941 in Manila Polly had kept her figure and had remained around one hundred and twelve.

When she walked into his room in the hospital, Pappy's eyes narrowed as he looked her over. During the past few days since leaving Santo Tomas she had absorbed all the calories we could cram into her, but she still wouldn't have tipped the scales at more than ninety pounds. A little lump gathered in Pappy's throat but he covered it up and growled, "Look, Polly, I know I said I'd divorce you if you didn't watch your diet, but hell, you didn't have to overdo it."

Polly had one of those lumps in her throat, too. Her husband looked pathetic, tired, and drawn. She sensed that she and the children probably looked that way to Pappy. Like him, she tried to cover up her emotions and replied, "Never mind that now. Tell me where you have been for the past three years. I know where I've been."

They both brushed away a few tears and the whole family laughed happily at the old jokes. Nothing mattered now. They were together again.

With the arrival of Polly and the children Pappy for a while was a new man. He was so glad to see them, and there was so much to tell on both sides, that he didn't have time to think of his troubles. The stories of Pappy's part in the war took a prominent part in the daily recounting of the events of the past three years, and, as usual, the stories soon took on the vividness that only he could impart to them. The youngsters listened wide-eyed. Nathaniel, in particular, drank in every word, lost in admiration of his father. One day the boy was sitting cross-legged on the floor by Pappy's chair saying nothing — just listening. Pappy had evidently run low on his stories and reaching back in his memory told his famous story of landing on the whale in the Atlantic Ocean back in 1930 while on navy manoeuvres.

Nathaniel listened to the end, then got up and started to walk away.

"That does it, Dad," he said, "I believed all those other stories up to this one. Now I don't believe any of them."

18. ADJUSTMENT TO CIVIL LIFE

ABOUT THE middle of April 1945 the doctors decided to send Pappy back to the United States where he could get his arm treated by a specialist in neurosurgery. He was flown to San Francisco and sent to the army hospital at Auburn, near Sacramento. Polly and the children were to follow later as soon as passage was available on a troopship.

As soon as he arrived, Pappy called his sister Jewell, in Texarkana. He told her that Polly and the children were in Australia waiting for boat passage and would not be home for at least another month. He said he was going to be sent to some hospital near San Francisco to have his arm operated on and would let her know as soon as he was located. His voice sounded so unnatural to Jewell that when he phoned a few days later to tell her that he was in Auburn and would be operated on the following week, she decided to go out there to be with her favourite brother, at least until Polly and the children arrived.

Jewell got an airplane ride as far as Dallas where military priority put her off. There were no Pullman reservations available but that didn't stop the determined Jewell. She rode a day coach all the way to San Francisco, then took a bus to Auburn, paused long enough to clean up at the local hotel, and went out to the hospital to see her brother.

Pappy needed cheering up. He was suffering intense pain and had lost a lot of weight. Jewell was shocked at the way he looked and asked him what she could do to help out. Pappy begged her to stay with him until Polly and the rest of the family arrived and then to take the children home with her. As soon as he recovered from the operation enough to get convalescent leave, he and Polly would follow them. Jewell promised she would stay around and take care of the youngsters when they arrived.

It was the third of May before Polly landed at Los Angeles from the troopship. Train reservations were not available, but "Dutch" Kindelberger, the president of North American Aviation in Los Angeles, supplied a station wagon and solved their transportation problem. Jewell took the children home to Texarkana and two weeks later Polly and Pappy joined them for a short visit, and then the whole family moved back to the old home in Pensacola.

The operation on Pappy's arm had helped some but was far from a complete success. He still suffered a lot of pain and had to carry the arm in a sling. By this time the hand had wasted away so much that the fingers looked almost like claws and had lost nearly all their strength. Worse than anything, however, was the effect on Pappy's morale of the inactivity and feeling of uselessness. He made up his mind that he was not going to be an invalid. There was work to be done. The war was now over and Philippine Air Lines had to be reorganized and started up again. Letters, wires, and telephone calls to everyone he knew from Washington to Tokyo finally got him transferred back to Manila in September 1945, where, shortly afterward, he was discharged from active duty and placed on reserve. The younger boy Nathaniel, now fifteen, went back with him. Paul entered the University of Missouri. Polly and the two girls, Connie, twenty-one, and Julie, nineteen, remained in Pensacola waiting for Pappy to get settled. He said he would need some time to straighten the affairs of the Philippine Air Lines but would send for them as soon as he could afford it.

Dan Stickle, his old maintenance man, who had been discharged from the Air Force as soon as the war ended, came back to help his old friend and boss. Pappy as vice-president in charge of operations and Dan as chief of maintenance and engineering put the company back in business. Dan's maintenance manuals and overhaul procedures that he put into effect at that time are still in use. Surplus cargo airplanes were acquired from the Army and remodelled for passenger carrying, and pilots and mechanics hired and trained. In December 1945 service in the Philippines was inaugurated for the first time since the war and a year later PAL's operations were extended to Hong Kong and Saigon, Indo-China.

Pappy, who by this time was practically living at the army hospital at Fort McKinley, left to attend the opening ceremonies and then went back to bed. In spite of almost continual suffering he never mentioned his troubles in his letters to Polly but gave as his excuse for not sending for her that he couldn't afford it just yet.

By the spring of 1947 Philippine Air Lines had decided to expand its services to the United States and Pappy came back to negotiate for purchase of aircraft with range enough to make the long Pacific hops.

I ran into him in Washington during this trip. He was still carrying his arm in a sling but every once in a while would slip it out and start squeezing a little rubber ball to get the blood circulating in his hand and build up the strength in his fingers. He still had a lot of pain and was even more nervous and fidgety than during the war, but he had gained back some weight and was quite evidently trying to keep so busy that he would forget about his arm.

As usual, Pappy had a scheme to propose. He wanted me to resign from the Air Force and migrate to Manila where I would head a company incorporating Philippine Air Lines, a maintenance, repair, and supply depot, and a bartering organization. This last was an essential in doing business in the Orient. Pappy believed the proposed company would finally have a monopoly of all air operations in the Far East and that American equipment would take over because of the ease of getting spare parts and overhaul of engines and aircraft at a convenient place such as Manila.

I don't know whether the directors of Philippine Air Lines or the Philippine Government, which owned 51 per cent of the stock, had told Pappy to approach me on the proposition, but in any event I told Pappy I was not interested. I was busy trying to get the Strategic Air Command organized and trained. In our haste to demobilize at the close of World War II we had let our long-range bomber capability drop to a handful of aircraft and a few fighter and bomber groups either on paper or equipped with obsolete airplanes. We were frantically modernizing old World War II airplanes and training flying and ground crews to utilize them. I still shudder to think of what would have happened if we had been forced into a war with the Reds at that time. We would have put up a fight but there would have been a long list of posthumous decorations.

That summer Pappy went back to Manila. Polly, Julie, and Paul, who had completed two years at the university, went with him. Nathaniel, in the meantime, had remained in Manila to learn something about airline operations. Connie, the eldest, had been married the previous year and now, as Mrs. Ralph Minor, had settled down in Dallas, Texas.

That fall Dan Stickle, who still had not fully recovered from the effects of three years' mistreatment as a Jap prisoner, went back to the United States for a check-up. He never returned to Manila. The doctors advised against it. Dan is now married and living in Dallas, Texas.

During October I was in the Philippines making an inspection of air bases before continuing on to Japan for a conference with General MacArthur. I didn't see Pappy, as he was away from Manila on business for Philippine Air Lines, but when I paid a courtesy call on President Rojas one of the first subjects discussed brought his name into the picture.

It seemed that Gunn and some local business associates had bought a lot of salvage from the war-surplus materials at Nichols Field just outside Manila. Most of the stuff was just junk. Labels had washed off many of the boxes and cases that had been stored in the open for more than two years. Metal parts were rusted and corroded and anything made of cloth had rotted away during the rainy season. Pappy figured that at a price of around one cent a pound they couldn't lose much and that he might be able to reclaim enough of the airplane and engine parts and instruments to make a decent profit.

In unpacking one of the crates he found a number of sets of the equipment known as IFF or "Identification Friend or Foe" which was installed on all our aircraft during the war. This equipment emitted a radio code signal which let us know whether the airplane approaching our airdromes was one of our own or some Jap trying to sneak up on us. By this time, although it was still classified as "secret," everyone in the world had IFF. We had furnished it to the Russians and to the Chinese forces of Chiang Kai-shek who were still fighting Mao's Communist armies. It apparently didn't dawn on Pappy that he might be violating any army or navy regulations by selling the IFF he had found among the junk he had acquired. The Chinese Nationalists were the only people then at war so to Pappy they were potential customers.

He had just about started negotiations when word of his possession of the equipment came to General Whitehead commanding the Far East Air Forces. Whitehead couldn't ignore the fact that Pappy was trying to sell secret equipment of the United States Army to a foreign power. Regardless of his affection for Pappy and his private opinion about the IFF still being so classified, he felt that he had to take action. A detail of troops suddenly appeared at Pappy's warehouse, seized the equipment, and carted it off to the air base at Clark Field.

Rojas said he didn't know how important the IFF equipment was but he could understand the anxiety of the United States Army to safeguard its military secrets. He didn't want to make an issue of the matter, but since the Republic of the Philippines was now a sovereign nation he believed that the matter should have been handled through him. Philippine citizens who had innocently come into possession of this equipment were not guilty of any crime and their property which they had purchased from the United States Army should not have been seized without proper authority.

I couldn't help but agree with him. I promised to look into the matter on my return to Washington. When I got back I checked it with the Signal Corps and steps were taken to declassify the IFF from its former "secret" designation. What was done about the stuff in the Philippines I never found out. Eventually I just put it down as another one of those things that always seemed to happen whenever Pappy Gunn was involved.

In the spring of 1948 the whole family returned to the United States. Pappy's arm was getting worse and he said that this time if the doctors couldn't fix it he'd have it cut off. I advised him to see an old friend of mine, Dr. James Walker, an orthopaedic surgeon in Dayton, Ohio. I had a lot of faith in Jim and believed that he would either fix Pappy's arm or tell him where the job could be done. Walker advised Pappy to see a Dr. Livingston at the Lahey Clinic in Boston.

The repair job turned out quite well. Nerves, arteries, and muscles were spliced and straightened out enough so that Pappy forgot about wanting to have an amputation. The arm never would be as good as new but pain was greatly relieved, a fair measure of circulation restored, and soon the colour began to return and the hand became of some use. Pappy still carried around his little rubber ball which hung on a string inside his sleeve. It probably helped by exercising the fingers, but more important it gave Pappy something to absorb his overabundant nervous energy. It soon became a sort of trade-mark and I think that after a while Pappy really depended on that little rubber ball for relaxation.

Because of his operation and business Pappy and the family stayed in the United States a little more than six months before returning to Manila in late 1948. Paul went back to the University of Missouri to finish his course in journalism.

The Army had made Pappy a colonel on March 4, 1946, and had placed him in the reserve on inactive duty, which meant no money. It didn't seem right to me, so every time I got a chance around the Pentagon, I recommended a physical-disability retirement which would give him three quarters of his old base pay. It wasn't a lot of money but it would help keep a nice family together. On June 30, 1948, the Army came through and Pappy was given a physical-disability retirement as a full colonel.

19. PAPPY AND THE HUKS

IT WAS the fall of 1950 when I next saw Pappy. I had been to Australia on a good-will mission carrying a message from President Truman to the Australian prime minister, Mr. Menzies, and presenting some United States Air Force flags to the Royal Australian Air Force which had served under me during the Pacific War. From Australia I flew to Manila on my way to Japan where I was to confer with my old commander, General Douglas MacArthur.

I landed just after dark at Clark Field, about sixty miles north of Manila. Waiting to meet me were Major General "Gene" Eubank, an old friend dating back to World War I, Major General Kangleon, the Philippine secretary of defence who as leader of the guerrillas on Leyte had welcomed us when we landed there in October 1944; Colonel Peralta, the old guerrilla leader on Panay, who was now a senator; Brigadier General Cruz, chief of the Philippine Air Force, and Pappy Gunn still clenching and unclenching his left hand around the little rubber ball.

They were all old favourites of mine and after dinner at the Officers' Club we settled down to reminiscing about the last war and speculating on the trouble then going on in Korea. Pappy said he wished the Air Force would put me in command and take him with me as he had some new ideas about improving our airplanes and I was the only one that had sense enough to listen to them.

About midnight the Filipinos all left to fly back to Manila, inviting Pappy to go along with them. Pappy said, "No, I drove my car up here and I'm driving it back tonight."

They all remonstrated with him as the Hukbalahaps, or "Huks," as they were generally called, were in rebellion against the Philippine Government and at night patrolled the roads between Clark Field and Manila. Rojas had died a few months before and Quirino, the former vice-president who had succeeded him, was having a hard time trying to keep the Huks under any kind of control. During the war they had been a guerrilla organization fighting on the main island of Luzon. In fact, the name Hukbalahap means in Tagalog, the native language, "Society for Killing Japs." At the end of the war they had degenerated into a bandit outfit and finally into a

Communist-led organization with the avowed aims of throwing out all Americans and becoming pals of their brethren in Moscow.

The next day I flew to Manila to have lunch with Ramon Magsaysay who was being groomed to take Kangleon's place as secretary of defence as the latter was resigning to go back to run his plantation on Leyte.

As I came into Magsaysay's office he greeted me with, "It could only happen to Pappy Gunn." I asked him what he meant. "General Kenney," he replied, "you must be the only man in Manila who doesn't know what happened to Pappy last night. Why, the story is all over town."

Pappy had said good night to us the night before and had headed his car toward Manila. About halfway to the city he had come upon a road block with several of the rebel Huks standing there on guard. It didn't disturb Pappy, who started to drive around the obstruction without paying any attention to the shouts to halt until a couple of shots tore through the back of the car and bored two ugly-looking holes in his windshield.

Mad as a hornet, Pappy jammed on the brakes, jumped out of the car, and running up to the nearest Huk — who was holding a smoking tommy gun — smashed him under the chin with a haymaker right that knocked him cold. Pappy then turned to the other astounded bandits and yelled, "Get the several blanks out of my way you blank, profane, and obscene thugs of doubtful ancestry. I'm Colonel Gunn on my way to Manila and I don't intend to have any more of you blanks stop me."

He got in his car and drove off hurling a final word back to them that while they were standing around there making nuisances of themselves they could figure out who was going to pay for his windshield.

Magsaysay finished his story and said, "If I ever tried to get away with anything like that I would have wound up with twenty bullet holes in me." He was right. It could happen only to Pappy Gunn.

Polly and Julie came back home in May 1950. Pappy arranged for them to go home by way of Europe where he wanted them to do some touring to see something of the world besides the Southwest Pacific. They didn't know it but it was to be the last time they would see Pappy alive.

Each year Polly would get her passport renewed for the return to the Philippines but something always seemed to post-pone the trip. All four of the children began to have troubles that stemmed from the long period of malnutrition while they were interned in the Jap prison at Santo Tomas.

In late 1950 and part of 1951 Connie's anaemic condition made her first pregnancy so serious that Polly decided to stay with her until she was fully recovered.

The next spring Nathaniel developed a bad abscess in the upper part of his left lung and was flown back to the United States where he was operated on. The convalescence was long. Once again Polly postponed her return to Manila to look after him.

Paul, who graduated from college in 1950, continued to have trouble with his back which had been overstrained in the Japanese prison camp. When he complained, the Japs accused him of malingering and gave him still heavier loads to carry. Upon graduation from the university his number was up for military service but the examining doctors classified him as 4F.

When the Korean War broke out that summer, however, they decided that he was fit for service. In early 1951 he was inducted into the Army and sent to Korea, where he remained until 1955, when he was discharged and got a job in Tyler, Texas.

In the meantime Pappy had severed his connection with Philippine Air Lines and had organized a company of his own called the Philippine Aviation Development Company. He acquired some Cessnas, Beechcrafts, and DC-3's and began charter flying in the Islands of both passengers and freight, doing photographic mapping and maintenance and engine overhaul work for both the United States Air Force at Clark Field and the Philippine Air Force. His financial position for several years was none too good, and this fact was an additional reason for not getting Polly back to Manila.

Julie was married in November 1956 in Pensacola where Polly was living and where all her family could be present. Her husband was Victor Bonanno, whom Julie had met in Washington a few years before while they were both working for the same governmental department. After the wedding they returned to Arlington, Virginia, just across the river from the national capital. They still live there.

Pappy did not attend Julie's wedding. He gave as an excuse that the business of acting as manager, principal pilot, and superintendent of maintenance and engineering of his airline would not permit his leaving Manila at that time. I suspect, however, that he couldn't really afford the trip. Every dollar he could get hold of outside an allowance to Polly was going for equipment to increase the capacity of Philippine Aviation Development Company.

Until recently his last demonstration of the ingenuity that made him famous could be seen in his old shop at Nichols Field just southwest of Manila. He bought two two-seater advanced training planes as salvage from the Philippine Government. He then joined the two wing centre sections together, using the original outer wing panels of one of the planes, and built a new fuselage which would accommodate twelve passengers and a crew of two. Pappy was convinced that this airplane would not only prove successful but would be a most economical island-hopping means of air transport for the Philippines. It remains as another monument to his ingenuity and creativeness.

On the afternoon of October 11, 1957, Pappy was flying a load of lumber-company executives and engineers in a twin-engined Beechcraft from Manila up to the Cagayan Valley in north-eastern Luzon to look over a timber tract. On the return flight about ten minutes out of Manila he ran into a tropical downpour. The combination of a solid wall of rain, heavy turbulence, and one engine quitting made Pappy decide to turn around and attempt an emergency landing. Trying to turn at low altitude into a small clearing with a dead engine and in rough air, he hooked a wing on a palm tree, crashed, and burned. There were no survivors. One of his passengers was young Carlos "Mike" Romulo, the son of General Carlos Romulo the Philippine ambassador to the United States and representative at the United Nations.

Fourteen years before, when visiting his sister Jewell during his trip home in 1943, Pappy had said that his dream was to stay active in the flying game as long as he lived and that when the time came, as it eventually does to all mankind, he preferred "to die with his boots on."

The dream was now over, but Pappy's wish had been fulfilled.

20. PAPPY'S LAST FLIGHT

POLLY WAS staying with her daughter Connie in Texas City, Texas, where she and her husband Ralph Minor had just moved a short time before from Dallas. Connie was having trouble with another pregnancy and Polly had come to help out. They hadn't yet gotten a telephone installed.

Word had come to the State Department from our embassy in Manila of Pappy's death. When unable to contact Polly, someone had the forethought to call her son Paul, in Tyler, Texas. Paul drove all that night to Texas City and brought the news to Polly ahead of the morning newspapers that had carried it. She seems to have had some sort of premonition, for she says that she had slept very badly all night and her fitful dreams had been a crazy kaleidoscope of Manila, the Jap bombings at the start of the war, and her life at Santo Tomas during the internment mixed up with remembered extracts of letters that Pappy had written her.

Paul also told Nathaniel, who was in Texas City visiting his mother and Connie, that the American embassy had urged that someone go to Manila immediately to take over the Philippine Aviation Development Company as all the property was under guard and all operations at a standstill until someone could take over responsibility for it. Paul promised that if Nate would leave immediately he would follow right after the funeral and help his brother run Pappy's old company. A wire was sent to Colonel Haskins, the base commander at Clark Field, that Nate was on the way and that the family wished the body sent to Pensacola, Florida, for interment in the nearby National Cemetery at Fort Barrancas. Nate left for Manila on October 13, 1957, and arrived just before Pappy's body was shipped home.

"Doc" John Gilmore, now a reserve Air Force colonel, practicing medicine in Santa Monica, California, and an old friend of Pappy in the 3rd Attack Group, was designated by the Air Force to accompany the body to its final resting place.

I asked "Doc" to tell me the story of his last association with Pappy. Here is the remarkable sequence of events that proved to be typical of the whole life of the man this book is about.

"After Pappy's death," says Doc, "I talked to the Gunn brothers in Tyler several times and was told that Nate would be going through Los Angeles on his way to Manila. I met him at Los Angeles International Airport and subsequently got him off to Manila via Pan American Airways.

"About eight days later I received a wire from the commanding general at Clark Field in the Philippines stating that Colonel Gunn's body was being shipped via Military Air Transport Service to Travis Air Force Base about eighty miles north of San Francisco, where it would be at the Jones Mortuary at Suisan, California, assigned to me. This caused very little thought on my part as I figured it was just some kind of formality. Little did I realize that Pappy on his last of many flights over the Pacific was traveling unauthorized, incognito, without orders, and contrary to all regulations. This would have pleased Pappy if he had known about it. Somehow I think he did. I hope so, anyway.

"Well, to keep things on an even keel I called the mortician at Suisan and suggested that when the body arrived it be placed on the next plane for Pensacola, Florida. He advised me that it would be many days and perhaps weeks before the body arrived, as it might be taken off the flight several times for high priority cargo. He promised to call me on its arrival.

"Nearly a week later the mortician at Suisan called me and said that the body had arrived. I suggested again that he send it on to Pensacola. He said he could only send it to New Orleans by train, as no air transport was authorized for anyone. He also stated that he could not send the body anywhere at this time as it was in a shipping case and someone would have to pick out and purchase a casket. He further stated that Colonel Gunn was retired personnel and was authorized nothing. I saw we were getting nowhere fast so I called Washington. I talked with a half-a-dozen people during the next day and a half explaining the situation and getting madder all the time as I tried to argue someone into taking action.

"The family by now had made arrangements for Pappy's funeral at the National Cemetery at Fort Barrancas the coming Monday. It was now Thursday morning. I called the mortician and selected a casket by telephone. This proved to be easy, as I got one that is used by civilian contractors for deceased military personnel. It proved to be quite nice.

"In a few hours I received a call from Washington that an airplane would arrive at Travis Air Force Base on Friday from Enid, Oklahoma, to pick up Colonel Gunn's body and deliver it to Pensacola. Things were moving well now. The next day I called Travis, talked to the operations officer, and instructed him to put the body on the airplane, turn it around, and head directly for Florida. That would just about allow enough time for delays along the route and still get there in time for the funeral. My personal affairs made it extremely difficult to arrange things so that I could attend the funeral but I felt that I had taken care of things pretty well for my old buddy and that I would fly to Florida Sunday and see him on his way. This was Friday.

"Saturday afternoon my thoughts were dwelling on Pappy being en route to his final resting place and on his last flight, thinking over his career, the many things he had done, and what a grand guy he really was. At this moment the phone rang. It was the mortuary officer at Travis Air Force Base. He stated that the airplane had arrived and that they were awaiting me to attend as escort. I explained my situation and asked to have the pilot call me. In a few minutes he called. I instructed him to put the body on the airplane and get going. He stated that he had orders to pick me up as escort with the body and he wasn't going to put it on board unless the escort was there. I suggested he call his commanding officer in Enid, Oklahoma. It was now 5:00 p.m. Saturday. Nothing was moving.

"I called 'Jock' Henebry the old 3rd Attack Group commander in New Guinea, a former buddy of Pappy and now an Air Force reserve brigadier general. Perhaps he could give me some help. He promised to do some telephoning to Washington.

"As I finished talking to Jock, the commanding officer at Travis called me and instructed me to get up there right away. He apparently thought that I was an officer on active duty in southern California. I proceeded to tell him that I had no official orders to go anywhere and that it seemed very simple to me to put the body on the airplane and get going. He said he didn't know how Pappy's body ever got there in the first place. He had travelled unauthorized across the Pacific and now there was an unauthorized airplane there to pick him up. There were no orders for anything and no authorization for anything. He had never handled a situation like this but he did know one thing, that a lot of phone calls had come in from Washington concerning this Colonel Gunn. He didn't know who Gunn was but the situation had received more personal attention from the brass in Washington than any other deceased personnel that had ever passed through Travis including any and all generals. He was handling the situation with kid gloves and he was damned if he would let the body move out without me as an escort.

"With this light thrown on the matter, I asked him to have a staff car at the San Francisco Airport to meet the ten-thirty plane that night and promised that I would be on it. I arrived in San Francisco on schedule, and drove the eighty miles to Travis, arriving about one o'clock Sunday morning. I went directly to the operations office where I was told that the body was in the mailroom ready for departure and that the pilot had scheduled an 8:00 a.m. take-off. I awakened the pilot and told him to meet me with his crew at the mess hall when it opened at 5:00 a.m. We had breakfast, but found we could get no flight lunches until 7: 00 a.m. We immediately loaded the body. I told the crew they would have to take off without flight lunches. The pilot added that we had all better get a last drink of water, as there was none on the airplane.

"We took off at 6:00 a.m. and flew nine hours to Enid, Oklahoma, without food or water and with very few words between me and the pilot. At Enid we switched to another plane and crew and arrived without further event at Pensacola, Florida, about 11:00 p.m. Sunday.

"I forgot to say that when I arrived at Travis I called the commanding officer and asked for orders to cover the trip. He informed me that this whole thing was so irregular that he couldn't cut orders on me and if we had to make an emergency landing en route I would just have to look after myself and ramrod the thing through.

"This was Pappy 's last flight, and I am sure he would have enjoyed every irregular minute of the entire trip.

"The funeral was held on schedule the next afternoon. I received the flag which covered the casket and presented it to Pappy's widow, Polly Gunn — the last formality in placing to rest a great guy."

Besides Polly and Doc at Barrancas there was Jock Henebry, General Jared Crabb, who headed the 5th Bomber Command from New Guinea to the Philippines, Dan Stickle, Julie, and Paul. Connie wanted to be there. She had driven through from Texas City with her mother and Paul to attend the funeral but on that afternoon she was in the hospital with a premature baby and couldn't make it.

The saga had ended much along the same lines that Pappy had lived it. Of course even the end had to be different, and we should have expected it to be that way. As a retired Air Force officer and a Mason, he was buried in a navy cemetery with an Air Force firing squad in attendance, and his last rites were performed by a Catholic chaplain from the Navy.

We didn't bury an ordinary man that day — we buried Pappy Gunn.

Made in the USA
San Bernardino, CA
08 October 2017